# CHANGE IN THE LIFESTYLE AMONG IRANIAN URBAN WOMEN

# CHANGE IN THE LIFESTYLE AMONG IRANIAN URBAN WOMEN

## A Case Study of Tonekabon, Iran

Dr Marzieh Gorjiposhti
Dr Anjali Kurane

KALPAZ

Change in the Lifestyle Among Iranian Urban Women—
*A Case Study of Tonekabon, Iran*



ISBN: 978-81-7835-930-4



Published in 2013 in India by
Kalpaz Publications
C-30, Satyawati Nagar,
Delhi-110052
E-mail: kalpaz@hotmail.com
Phone : 9212729499

*Lasser Type Setting* : Quick Media, Delhi
*Printed at* : Chawla Offset Printers, Delhi

*Dedicated*

*to*

*Our Dear Parents*

## Contents

## Acknowledgements

During our research a number of people extended their ungrudging support in various ways. We are sincerely grateful to them who have devoted their time and effort, shared their ideas and opinions to help us to execute the work in good time. We are highly indebted to them for their persistent, constant encouragement, in-depth and lively technical discussions, and for critically and patiently improving this dissertation.

We are also obliged to the co-operation and assistance from the Department of Anthropology and Sociology and from the Library of Faculty of Social Science in Tehran University, public library and government of Tonekabon city. We express our thanks to staff member of Jaykar Library; Sociology Library, Women Studies Library and Department of Anthropology of Pune University.

A few names however need special mention such as Mr. Sayyed Mohammad Karimi Behbahani, Mrs. Jyothi Shetty, Mr. Shantanu Ozarkar, Mr Athokpam Bijesh Kumar, Mr. Omid Varzande, Dr. Bakhtiar Sajadi, Dr. Ali Shagho-el Islami, and Ms. Ayda Rahmani for their cooperation and support.

We are highly indebted to our family members for their patience and ungrudging support throughout this long and difficult operation. Their support and cooperation made this study possible.

We also thank all our respondents who shared their life time experiences and provide necessary and valuable information to us.

Finally, we would like to thank all whose direct and indirect support helped us completing our work in time.

# 1
# Introduction

## I. INTRODUCTION

According to Noah Webster, (1963) "change" means to be altered; to become different; to undergo variation; to be partially or wholly transformed; as, men sometimes change for the better. In other words, any variation or alteration in form, state, quality, or essence; or, a passing from one state or form to another is called change. Gerald Zaltman (1977:13) stated that "Change may take a variety of forms. Change may simply be an idea or concept that may or may not lead to a different practice and may or may not manifest itself in a physical product or service."

Anjali Kurane (2002) says that in this process there is transformation in socio-cultural values, socio-cultural behaviours, traditional thought pattern and attitude, worldview, style of life. Developments like pread of education, participation in the politics, political independence, industrialization, urbanization, development and spreading of banking organization, rapid development in transformation and communication, and so on have brought and necessitated the transformations among men and his social relationship and society. Further she says that "in the end of 19th century and beginning of the 20th century, when society experienced rapid changes, anthropologists were preoccupied with studying the problem of the process of change by which this transformation has taken place. Many social scientists such as Comte, J. S. Mill, Spencer, Marx, Gordon Childe, and MacIver have analyzed this transformation of the society. Today, the study and analysis of the nature of, and resistance to, the transformations have become an important and necessary problem".

Kinsley Devis (1950) used the terms "social change" versus "cultural change". He says, "Social change means alteration in the social organization". Social change thus focuses only on a part of essentially broader category that is "culture", whereas cultural change embraces all the changes occurring in any branch of culture including art, science, technology, philosophy etc, as well as changes in the forms and rules of social organization.

## II. CHANGE IN "LIFESTYLE"

Johanne Charbonneau, Madeleine Gauthier, (2002:349-617) said that "A 'lifestyle' is something located at a junction between 'styles of living' and 'living conditions'. Whereas styles of living are determined through personal choices and tastes, and point up the freedom to take decisions affecting one's daily life, living conditions may be seen more as boundaries, marking out the limits of such freedom. These boundaries are defined both by the social context and by the individuals themselves. The relationship between the impact of the objective determinants of individual behaviour and the role played by the subjects as autonomous beings in control of their destiny is a favorite and constant theme of major debate in the social sciences".

"Lifestyle" is a collection of interpretations, values, behaviours, modes and different tastes in different subjects from music to art and TV, and to style of gardening, decoration, furniture..."Lifestyle" is not a personal behaviour, so it is not something unusual, but most of the people believe they should choose their "Lifestyle" freely.

Lifestyle" is related to personal identity, because it tells a special story that a person chooses for his/her own identity against others and requires daily decision making on how to dress, consume, work and spending leisure time. Concept of

"Lifestyle" means adaptation of one style approach in life. For instance it is important for the people to be famous like a singer. He even eats Thai food, painting their home with special colour or take recreation/to amuse at home, not outside. Most of the time, the elements of "Lifestyle" are exposed in forms that many people share. In other words, social groups all follow one lifestyle.

T.V., newspaper, internet, magazines and so on give us the new image of lifestyle, so media is very important today. In this regard G.S. Ghurge (1963:279) said that "Most of us know, though many of us do not possess one, what style means in writing, but Kroeber's 'style' is not that specific mode of writing which is individual. It is a socio-cultural phenomenon. The most sensitive though least objectifiable indicator of a civilization is style, especially in the fine arts, but also, in a broad way, in decoration, dress and food".

Anthony .J. Veal (2001) stated the concept of "lifestyle" has a long history in numerous disciplines and fields of study, including leisure studies. But in the latter context, despite a growing literature, it has generally been marginalized from the mainstream of theoretical debate and empirical enquiry.

Lifestyle is like identity, the lifestyle of people is a part of their identity. David Chaney (1996) says, "Lifestyle is a very important source of identity"; that means, it is important what you wear, what carpet you have and what is your idea about music and they are as important as belonging to a social cast in old days.

Ogburn (1966) in his extensive studies of change phenomena, separated two aspects of the activities of society's members: the material and socio-cultural aspects. He believes that the material culture unfolds and changes according to the principle of accumulation, which simply means that new discoveries and inventions build upon past ones. However, the principle does not apply to other aspects of culture such as values, religious beliefs, art, law, traditions and education which don't develop cumulatively but rather are replaced by new ones. His central hypothesis therefore is that changes in material culture proceed at a faster rate than changes in adaptive culture – customs, beliefs, philosophies, laws and government and the result is continues maladjustment between two types of culture (Smelser, 1967). The rapid rate of development in material culture causes social maladjustment and pressures for change in the adaptor structures.

## III. LIFESTYLE AND MODERNIZATION

The process of modernization has affects on the Lifestyle. Recent scholars such as Tim Woods (2000) say that modernization as a process also affects the way a society thinks, its attitudes, beliefs, food, dress habits, and cultural patterns at the level of individuals, and as the individuals can be seen as units of the society, through them society at large is also affected.

"Modernization" refers to a kind of lifestyle or social construction, as Giddens puts it. Modern technology is an inseparable part of people's daily life. Therefore, we can claim that modern technology has also caused change in lifestyle. Innovation is a phenomenon that is mostly specific of higher social class or middle class.

The term "modernization" originally referred to the contrast and transition between modernity and tradition based on agriculture and modern society based on commerce and industry. Modernization can be seen as the general mechanism by which the social transformation from agricultural domination by trade and industry takes place, and the permanent continuation of this process. The difference between modernizing and traditional societies is profound being the difference between simple static structure and complex dynamic process.

K.N. Jha (1985:4) says, "The term modernization is used by common man in every day life and the words like modernity, modernism and modern are commonly used. But some times the term modernization is not correctly understood and refers simply to the acceptance of modern tools and equipment and to becoming westernized in dress pattern and overt behaviour. But this concept of modernization is not only a change in the material culture of a group or the material position of an individual, it is also system and ideological framework. It is also concerned with a change in belief system and the ideological framework. This means that it does not refer only to the changes in behaviour but also to a change in the inner state of mind [thought]... Modernization means development of modern approach and outlook and adoption of modernity in everyday life. But modernity does not mean only abandonment of religious views or only acceptance of modern tools and equipments. Modernity is something more than that. It is a complex phenomenon involving the development of rational outlook and acceptance of realities and facts in the context of scientific value. It refers to an inherent change in a particular direction for attaining modernity. Hence, modernization is a complex process of social change'.

The process of modernization presents members of the modernizing society a great many choices of new beliefs, values, behaviour patterns and habits to choose from. They have to make new choices regarding dress, the language they speak, and the food they eat, and these choices often result in social, culture and emotional conflict.

Some theorists have expanded views regarding lifestyle based on the notion of modern and post-modern society. David Chaney (1996), in his book entitled *"Lifestyle"*, states that lifestyle and its debate belongs to the modern era, when people were using the concept of lifestyle to justify their deeds and their behaviours. People use the word "lifestyle" in their daily life and nobody is expected to ask for an explanation. It is supposed to help understanding each other. It is to mention that not everybody necessarily follows a lifestyle. In his view, lifestyle is a part of people's daily life in the modern society that separates those who belong to the society from outsiders.

In the modern societies, global cultural development and the growth of modernism and post-modernism have caused class distinctions. For instance, specific characteristics are considered for higher social class and the new middle class. According to Anthony Veal (2002), in the post modern conditions which are characterized by a rapidly changing cultural environment, the base for constructing a lifestyle has become unstable; henceforth, that lifestyle itself would be unstable. He looks at this fact as threatening or, in his own words, likely to wreak "devastation across leisure." The western industrial revolution has produced several phenomena which have in turn destabilized the norms. These include urbanization, industrialization, the boom and slump of national economics, the changes in technology, and certainly wars, changes in cultural and social mores. Individuals face changes of partners, migration and house-moving, change of job, etc., to varying degrees.

Modernization also effects on Iranian society, such as: people's behaviours, beliefs and values. Moreover influences on their dress pattern and equipment, especially in young generation. Even younger people in traditional families who were loyal to the old customs changed their lifestyle as a result of modernization. Therefore in the present study to understand modernization in different aspect of culture, the researcher has focused on the various variables of material and non material culture.

In material culture, the researcher selected different variables such as:

(a) *Leisure time activities*, such as visit to or amount of time they spend in gym, body building clubs, cinema, public library, festivals, museum, concert hall, exhibition, park, historical places, tourist place, voyage, hobbies, restaurant, fast food restaurants, coffee shops, social work; visiting such as: visiting neighbours, visiting clubs, visiting different organizations, visiting skin clinic, attending party, chatting parties, visiting relatives, organized games at home, listening to radio, reading newspaper or magazine, recreation with children; other activities such as: sewing, knitting, embroidery work, religious activity, study, chess and rest.

(b) *Use of body management* such as; daily bath, plastic surgery, hair cutting, visiting beauty parlour, make up.

(c) *Personal habits* are; food/nutrition, hygiene, decoration of house, time of sleep, daily work time, taste, buying cloths, and smoking.

(d) *Use of mass media* such as; reading magazine and newspaper, watching T.V, cinema, listening to radio, music, use of computer and Internet.

(e) *Socio-economic indicators*; for instance, level of education, nature of occupation, income, and financial independence.

In non material culture, researcher has focused on attitude towards vital characteristics of women, and women beliefs on some traditional ceremonies such as; Norooz, their believes on some traditional customs in marriage such as; Khastegary, Namzadi, Aghd, Mahrieh and Sherbahaa.

## IV. LIFESTYLE AND LEISURE TIME ACTIVITIES

Leisure time activity is one of the most important factors of studying the change in Lifestyle.

Rojek draws on anthropological sources and classic leisure studies sources to argue for the crucial relationship between culture and leisure activity. He states: (2000, p.115) "Human culture did not begin with the need to work, it began with language, dancing, laughing, acting, mimicking, ritual and activity of play forms". He also believed, the combination of dress style, hairstyle, speech, music and dance tastes and attitude; that characterize such groups can be seen as the rules of performance of the group.

Leisure can happen in family activities or out of the family. Parker (1976:79) said, "The extent to which leisure has been spent within the circle of the family has changed during the course of history. Today a family is still a primary source of developing leisure attitudes of its young members, although other influences compete with those of the family in shaping leisure behaviour. There are differences between the various social classes in respect of the part played by the family in the leisure activities of its members and in the degree to which leisure is spent in the home. The family –society's primary agent of socialization- provides a setting in which the attitudes of children are developed towards all major institutions, including recreation and leisure. He added leisure activities outside the home usually cost more (in travel, admission fees, etc.) than leisure spent inside the home. Cost is no doubt an important factor in explaining the greater participation rates of the middle class than the working class in nearly all forms of leisure activity. Many of the popular out-of-home forms of recreation, whether commercialized (the cinema, theatre, sports events) or social (golf, bridge, tennis, dinner parties) are designed primarily not for family- wide participation, but for individual or couple participation".

Leisure activities of the sexes are different. There are pronounced differences in the leisure patterns of males and females in any society. Parker (1976:86) believed that, "Many such differences reflect the differences in role which have historically been ascribed to men and women. The traditional, home-based existences of women, their lower educational status, their primary role as home-maker and mother, their second class legal status, the comparatively sheltered condition of adolescent women and the differences in standards regarding sexual activity have all played a part in accounting for the difference in the leisure of women and men".

The role of leisure can be the main source of an individual's identity. Anthony. J Veal (2000:364) quoted Robert's statement; "...the concept of lifestyle implies some sort of primacy for the role of leisure, and therefore concludes that if this primacy is denied then the validity of the lifestyle concept will be undermined. However, for most models of lifestyle, this is far from the case. Attempts at empirical operationalisation of lifestyle generally see leisure as just one component of the phenomenon, along with socio-economic and lifecycle position, geographical factors, occupation, consumption patterns, attitudes and so on. Thus, lifestyle, far from giving primacy to leisure, can be seen as a means of "decentring" leisure and viewing it as just one component of life."

Nowadays, in Iran, financial matters, education and occupation influence the way people spend their leisure time. It also has influence on women, particularly the way they spend their leisure time. Consequently, in the present study to understand lifestyle and leisure time activities, the researcher has focused on the following Kaplan's six categories of the leisure activity such as; sociability, association, game, art, movement, immobility, which have been studied. The respondents were asked a range of questions about the amount of time they spend doing leisure activities such as; gym, body building clubs, cinema, public library, festivals, museum, concert hall, exhibition, park, historical places, touristy place, voyage, hobbies, restaurant, fast food restaurants, coffee shops, social work, visiting such as: visiting neighbours, visiting clubs, visiting different organization, visiting skin clinic, attending to party, chatting parties, visiting relative, organized game at home, listening to radio, reading newspaper or magazine, recreation with children, other activities such as; sewing, knitting, embroidery work, religious activity, study, chess and rest.

## V. LIFESTYLE AND BODY MANAGEMENT

Women's management of body is one of the important factors for women in their lifestyle.

Bourdieu (1984:206) believed that, "as for the women of the dominant class, they derive a double assurance from their bodies. Believing, like petit-bourgeois women, in the value of beauty and the value of the effort to be beautiful, and so associating aesthetic value and moral value, they feel superior both in the intrinsic, natural beauty of their bodies and in the art of self-embellishment and everything they call *tenue*, a moral and aesthetic virtue which defines 'nature' negatively as sloppiness."

Giddens (1990) believed that, Women's extremist activities to control over their bodies and appearance is an active protest, and it gives them a sort of power. They try to provide a proper platform to prove their self identity.

Women change 'self' through lifestyle, consumption and so on. The desire for consumption originates from the fact that they feel in need of upgrading and advancement in the scene of society. Of course it is not just about women but from the aesthetics point of view, they are more interested in lifestyle, cosmetics, body management, delicacy, beauty, etc. Both the individual and the society are involved in the change of the lifestyle.

In Iran, management of body such as; plastic surgery for beauty has become a fashion for rich women. The make up of women is dependent on their job and social status. In the present study, the researcher has tried to understand body management by focusing on different variables such as; daily bath, plastic surgery, hair cutting, visiting beauty parlour and make up.

## VI. LIFESTYLE, HABITS AND THE SPACE

The important means of personal habits are food/ nutrition, hygiene, house, sleep, taste, work, clothes, and smoking.

Habits include both a generative principle of classifiable judgments and the incumbent classification system for them. But the habitus is defined by the interrelation of the capacity to produce classifiable practices and works, and the capacity to differentiate and appreciate these practices and products. That is taste Bourdieu (1984) classified habits as both structure and structuring structure. That is, habits is the principle of dividing into logical classes to perceive the social classes.

Class conditions are defined by intrinsic properties and from relational properties in the system of class conditions. This is also a system of differential positions—*i.e.*, by everything which distinguishes it from what it is not and especially from everything it is opposed to; social identity is defined and asserted through difference.

'Taste' is another factor which is necessary for lifestyles. Bordieu added that taste refers to the capacity to appropriate symbolically or materially a given class of objects or practices. A particular dimension of a lifestyle will symbolize with another, or with all others, and simultaneously symbolizes it/them. For example, a taste in food depends on the physiological effects of the food per class of food- i.e., strength, health and beauty.

Bordieu continued to mention about eating habits. When considered according to the type of food consumed, eating habits can not be separated from the whole lifestyle. Certainly, taken by it, when we consider food as a criterion, we will think of eating habits. And obviously, taste for a certain food enters the picture. This includes cooking and preparation and includes the national economy as well as the 'division of labour' between men and women.

Referring to space, a third factor, spaces defined by food and other preferences in a lifestyle are organized according to that same structure. In this case, they are arranged by the social space determined by volume and composition of capital.

Regarding lifestyle and mental built, Bourdieu believes that body and all its constituents are of major importance in the activities such as cooking, physical practices, wearing clothes, and mutual relationships. He talks about mental built as a collection of resources and situations that we carry along every where.

According to him, mental built shows how university professors, for instance, have different criteria and norms for the preference of a food, drink, sport and so on; on the other hand, the common criteria and norms we all have for the preference of more delicious food, a better drink and a more interesting sport etc, are shown in different ways. The food a worker eats-especially the way he eats- and the sport he practices and the way he does that, his political views and the way they are expressed are systematically much different from the way the chairperson of the company does the same since the mental built is different. Bourdieu shows that the social class plays a major role in the lifestyle and the mental built of the people.

He, then, has used different concepts regarding lifestyle. His main concern is the variety of aesthetic tastes, that is, the sense of making difference between different cultural and aesthetic products.

Bourdieu (1984) also states that "taste" is an action that makes people understand their position in the social system. Also, it makes the tastes of those who have same preferences close together and separates them from those who have different tastes. It lets people categorize themselves based on their taste.

In Bourdieu's view, taste – that categorizes individuals— is considered so significant in the concept of lifestyle, and relates culture, cultural products and taste.

Bourdieu (1984) considers culture as a sort of market in which people make cultural investment rather than economical investment.

Individuals are in search of distinction in their society. For example the soft drink that they prefer (Coke or an expensive brand), their car (Mercedes or an ordinary car) the newspaper they read (*New York Times* or *Yellow Paper*) etc. Therefore, he considers a mutual relationship between cultural products and taste; that is, change in the cultural products would lead to a change in the taste and vice versa.

According to the all above mentioned, tastes are temporary, and the challenges among different forces in the cultural field of old and new fashion would lead to a different social class. Taste is a chance to experience a social position and express views on that foundation. The unconscious unity of a class comes from the people's preferences in the most materialistic aspects of culture such as food, clothes, or furniture that are all based on their mental built.

Bourdieu offers two classes of taste: Free taste and General taste. Free taste refers to luxuries, art and higher class aesthetics, while General taste is concerned with clothes, furniture and aesthetics in lower class. For instance, (Cinema and/or DVDs), art gallery for higher class and TV for labour class; delicacy and gentleness of taste for higher class and noisiness for lower class, and so on.

Tarner and Gronow believe that Bourdieu considers taste as a social feature that lets people categorize each other.

Taste and its norms and criteria regarding lifestyle, is a new research area in the current decade in Iran. According to Zibili, women – more than men – are interested in change and variety in the lifestyle. But the changes occur in different levels based on the social levels. Empirical researches show that identity has much to do with lifestyle and its changes during the course of life.

Veblen made a survey on the role of women in the rich higher class families in America. S/He came to know that women mostly manage furniture, clothes and jewelleries. S/He criticizes the male-dominated society that has degraded women to housewives and mere users.

Therefore, in this study to understand lifestyle and habits, researcher has focused on the various variables such as: food/nutrition, hygiene, decoration of house, time of sleep, daily work time, taste, buying of clothes, and smoking.

## VII. LIFESTYLE AND SOCIO-ECONOMICS

Social Condition standing was a significant factor in leisure desire and participation. Reissman (1954) reports that the upper class participated more often and with a greater variety in leisure activities than did the lower class. The upper class simply belonged to more organizations, consequently acquiring more friends, read more popular literature, from novels to newspapers, and accordingly learned about more organizations to join and activities to do.

Bourdieu (1984:107) stated that, 'social class is not defined by a property, not even the most determinant one, such as the volume and composition of capital nor by a collection of properties of sex, age, social origin, ethnic origin- proportion of blacks and whites, for example, or natives and immigrants- income, educational level etc, nor even by a chain of properties strung out from a fundamental property (position in the relations of production) in a relation of cause and effect, conditioner and conditioned; but by the structure of relations between all the pertinent properties which gives its specific value to each of them and to the effects they exert on practices. So he said other factors age, sex, place of residence etc, impose on practices.'

The impact of education seems to lay not so much in increasing awareness and desire. Swimming, for example, is a cheap pastime which is relatively unpopular among the lower income groups and the fewer well- educated.

In Iran, the type of socio-economics is very influential in how people spend their free time. Therefore the present study is to understand lifestyle socio-economics and, researcher has taken different variables such as; level of education, nature of occupation, income, and financial independence.

## VIII. LIFESTYLE AND MASS MEDIA

Communication plays an important role in the lifestyle. Exposure to the mass media is an important variable in large scale directed social change and modernization in developing societies. Lerner (1966) said that, the mass media makes indispensable inputs to psycho-political life of transitional society via the mind and hearts of its people. It teaches people by depicting new and strange situations and familiarizes them with a range of opinions among which they can choose.

The function of mass media, however, is to open up the large masses in society to new information, new thoughts, new attitudes, and new aspirations which lead them to new achievement.

The mass media, such as newspapers and cinema, have played a major role in defining patterns of leisure for a population. Listening to the radio is a common form of leisure, especially among the popular classes who may or may not have a television and even among the youth. In the cities, mass media is more influential. In the city, large numbers of the population are exposed to various channels of communication.

With the development of television, mass communication has entered a pioneering stage in some countries. Of course, television also entertains and exposes viewers to socio-cultural events. Urbanites benefit tremendously from television: they gain new information and knowledge on hygiene, political affairs and overall modernity.

The reading of journals and magazines has come up along side with newspapers but one's educational level determines the reading of these. Newspapers are still most frequently read.

Today, mass media plays an important role in spending leisure time. Education and mass media have interdependent relationship, because educated people use mass media such as: computer, internet, etc. Therefore, in present study to understanding lifestyle and mass media, researcher has focused on different variables such as; reading magazine and newspaper, watching T.V, cinema, listening to radio and music, use of computer and Internet.

## IX. HISTORICAL BACKGROUND OF WOMEN IN IRAN

*Women's Movements in Iran Pre-Revolutionary and Post-Revolutionary :*

The beginning of women's activism in domestic politics began in the years 1906-1911, when the new bourgeoisie and the urban mass politics developed. In January 1907, a meeting was held in Tehran to establish girls' schools and ten resolutions were adopted. Other women in the city attempted to educate young girls and continued their efforts despite objections. In 1913 totally, 9 women's societies and 63 girls' schools had opened in the country.

The Pahlavi dynasty began with the ascension of Reza Shah in 1926. In 1931 women earned the right to request divorce under specific conditions (unspecified here) and women could marry at the age of fifteen. The Congress of Oriental Women opened in Tehran in 1932. In 1934, women's activities were legal but were controlled by the state. The Ministry of Education established the Kanoun-e Banouvan and began to implement reforms.

Two leading Iranian feminists, in the western sense, emerged in this period: Huma and Shams al Muluk. Huma organised demonstrations and was a writer and poet. Shams was the first teacher to teach unveiled girl students. Her classes were also co-educational.

In 1936, unveiling was compulsory by law and women were unofficially emancipated. Women could wear neither chador nor scarf publicly. Boys and girls were educated equally. Women were also admitted to Tehran University. They also became lecturers. During this period, Reza Shah had forcibly unveiled women. Higher Council of Women was established in 1949. By 1964, this Council was known as Organisation of Iranian Women. It had totally 349 branches, 113 centres and included 55 other organisations by 1978.

At the same time, in 1962, women were given suffrage. Family Law was ratified in 1968 and divorce was taken up in family courts. There were significant changes to divorce, polygamy and other affairs—the first wife's signature was needed for approval. Under this law polygamy was strictly limited and a man could no longer get a divorce by reciting "Talaq" [divorce] three times. Husbands and wives were required to appear for divorce together. Originally the husband received custody of children under Shia laws. Parsa was Iran's first woman minister. By 1975, a widow could claim protection of her children, following death of the father. In 1975, Mahnaz Afkhami was Iran's first woman minister for women's affairs.

After Islamic Revolution, Ayatollah Khomeini had advocated women's activity in government. But from 1980 till 1983, the Family Protection law was annulled and after the Iran-Iraq war, widows lost their right to custody of the children in favour of their husbands' families.

The women's press began in the 1980s and developed in the succeeding decade. *Zan e Ruz*, a weekly magazine, issued between 1984 and 1991, reported the views of women activists and advocated women's demands. Chief editor Shahla Sherkat quit *Zan* and founded *Zanan* in 1992. It was a similar weekly magazine with high quality of penmanship, and it addressed both women and men on women's oppression. Among effects, *Zanan* quotes from sections of the Holy Quran, which mentions the equality between men and women, and attempted to explain the inequality.

Yet the women's press, which had been active long before the revolution, played a major role in the resistance to restrictions on women; among significant restrictions which they fought was the annulment of the Family Protection Law. Women parliamentarians joined the protest against these restrictions. In addition, the magazine *Zan e Ruz* (1964) became a platform to support the protest after the revolution. Women deputies in the *majles* (parliament) added their own arguments.

When Khatami was in Ministry of Culture and Islamic Guidance, he reduced the restrictions on the press and scores of books by and about feminists have been published. In 1993, the first Asian games for Muslim women were initiated by Faezeh Hashemi. However, she was attacked for wearing 'immodest dress.'

Women's press, including magazines, featured stories about wives with despotic husbands who beat them, or about women's suicides and loss of children. *Zan e Ruz* held a campaign and during 1984-85 marriage contracts were extended by twelve conditions. These cited reasons for women to divorce. These conditions matched those already in the annulled law, and civil courts were started to handle the proceedings. With the rising number of war widows and the protest against the loss of child custody, the government passed a bill in 1985 allowing widow's custody of minor children. Ayatollah Khomeini supported this and other departures from the *sharia* (Islamic laws).

As of 1998, fifty two percent (52%) of students in universities were women and millions of women entered the work force due to economic downturns. Women were allowed to be judges although they do not have this title. In fact, the fifth *majlis* (parliament) has totally 13 women deputies out of 270. In addition, women in Iran have begun a movement questioning the interpretations of the Quran. Women in Iran recently have spoken out against the strict dress codes and rules meted out to them by mullahs (religious teachers). They have campaigned for inheritance rights and for the custody of their children. Women have continually modified their public dress and more publications featuring women are appearing.

From 1988, the government of Iran has initiated programs of education and public health, and among the world's most effective birth control programmes, which naturally affects women, especially those in the lower classes. The development in women's and girls' education is noticeable, though much of that growth began from the beginning of the twentieth century.

## X. SOCIO-CULTURAL, RELIGIOUS, ECONOMIC AND POLITICAL ACTIVITIES OF WOMEN

Before the revolution, women in general had less participation in social activities. The majority of women were housewives or did low work, i.e. they were as office secretary or typist and so on. But nowadays, with regard to high percentage of educated women, they have more roles in social activities. They have their role in decision-making in the government and even they have participation in the international activities to improve the country's social welfare.

Before the revolution, less number of women had participated in politics i.e., *majles* (parliament) election or other elections; but, nowadays we observe that more number of women participate in politics and they have important role in different areas, like *majles* election, government key posts and so on. Although still they are fighting for injustice and inequality of men and women in the society, they hope to find a way for better situation. For instance, in the war of Iraq against Iran, women played important roles and they had participated in the war the same as men did. Also they had important role in victory of Islamic revolution. They appeared in demonstrations in the street like their men for striking and fighting with injustice. Even nowadays they are fighting for any inequality and discrimination.

After the Islamic Revolution, the social and cultural activities of women increased. Since majority of people in Iran are Muslims and 50% of the population are women, the religious activities of women are more important. Women participated in both public and private activities. Public activities are performed in streets, mosques and in public places. Programs that are held at home and in private places are examples of private activities.

Also, one of the most important economic and social changes in recent decades which had most consequences in population was development of universal education, in general and women's education in particular. Education makes women powerful both for their own empowerment and development of their country to advance, because around half of the population in Iran is female.

In/before revolution, most of the ceremonies were in traditional style, e.g., in marriage ceremony all traditional rites and rituals must be followed and couples had to do all ceremonies one by one. Nowadays, because of modernity there are lots of changes in marriage ceremony. In Norooz, the ceremony has not changed more because it is referred to historical and cultural background of people from the Old Persian (more than 2500 years ago) and they accepted it as a national ceremony. Moreover they believe that they must do the ceremony as their fathers did.

There are some changes in wedding parties after the Islamic Revolution. Before Revolution, people used to celebrate wedding for five to seven days; but now, because of economical and political matters, they celebrate it just in a day.

## Leisure Time

Before the revolution, people used to spend their leisure time normally. They went to parks, visited their relatives and friends. And those people who had better financial condition had went for a trip to other cities, like North of Iran, for swimming in Caspian Sea or other historical and religious places. And women could swim in the sea with swimming clothes anywhere in the sea. But nowadays there are restrictions, especially for women and they can swim just in *tarhe salemsazi darya* area (those places which were determined by the government for swimming). Also, today, modernity had changed the people's lifestyle and leisure time. Computer and internet are used by young ladies and girls for pleasure and fun and they chat with their friends and relatives. Also younger girls play game on computer, play station and game houses.

Nowadays, the women's lifestyle have changed. Especially the young girls who like to wear western clothes: Also, body management has changed, i.e., young ladies use cosmetics, put on chemical dye colours on their hair, use tattoo, nose surgery, and so on.

The furniture of the house also has undergone some changes. Women try to make a harmony in the home furniture, i.e., in style, colours, etc.

## Clothes

Before Islamic revolution, as mentioned before, Reza Shah had forcibly unveiled women. In urban areas women had to wear coat, skirt, shirt, T-shirt, suit and also they used western clothes, but in rural areas women usually had to wear traditional clothes. The traditional clothes included scarf, blouse, *shalith* (a short creased skirt), vest, skirt, pant and *shawl* wrapped around the waist.

After the revolution, the form of clothes had changed. According to *Sharia* (Islamic laws) and government rules, women have to wear *mantoo* (a body-length religious tunic) and *shalwar* (trousers) and *maghnaa* (the ultimate *hijab* for head and neck in the Islamic Republic) or *chador* (an outer garment or open cloak worn by some Iranian women) in public. Of course, wearing the *chador* also was compulsory in some government offices and universities. In the first decade of revolution, the form of *mantoo* was long and usually it was black, brown or dark in colour. But nowadays the form of *mantoo* has changed to short and fits the body with different colours. Even women, especially younger ladies and girls, are eager to wear coat, skirt, blouse, shirt, T-shirt, suit and western clothes. But they are not allowed to wear these clothes in public, although in capital city, like Tehran, women are wearing long *doman* (skirt) and blouse with *shawl*.

## XI. STATEMENT OF PROBLEM

At present, the rate of modernization in Iran has been extremely rapid. Recently, there is emphasis on large-scale industrialization with enormous moderates being given to industry. This has been accompanied by flow of migration from rural to urban areas. Urban areas have been expanding rapidly.

With modernization and urbanization, many changes have been brought in the family structure, lifestyle and attitude. In urban areas it is very common for women to work or be employed outside the home. Modern women have a very different role model in their family. Their attitudes to lifestyle are modern. Modernization in urban society affects women's attitude toward "Lifestyle", socio-cultural and socio- economic activities.

In addition, Iranian women want equality, respect and the right to participate in all social, political and economic activities. They participate in all social activities and they change their lifestyle according to modern society although sometimes there may be some restrictions. Throughout the 20th Century, Iranian women have organized and fought for human and political rights.

In Iran, one of the most important economical and social changes in recent decades having impact on population was development of universal education, in general and women's education in particular. Nowadays Iranian women are aware that, education is one of the most influential factor to achieve gender equality and empowerment of women. Education is making Iranian women powerful both for their own empowerment and for their country to grow, because around half of the population in Iran is female. Of course it is difficult to get into the university because there are limited seats and lots of volunteers for university and moreover there is entrance exam. In spite of this, in recent years, 60 percent of those admitted in the universities are women. Iranian women have proved their abilities in the universities.

Education is increasing direct and indirect costs, and moreover increases the economic benefits of the Iranian women. The direct result is change of flow of capital within generations and decrease of demand for children. On the other hand, education is changing the approaches of the Iranian women. Education is changing the Iranian women's approaches to values, and beliefs and also encourages them to family planning and birth-control.

Iran does not utilize the resources of women workforce. Women are not promoted to managerial positions, many educated women are unemployed and few women are elected to parliament. There are a few limitations in the law to women for key posts and managerial position. Just a few women reach the managerial position even though there are many qualified women in from, so that we can have many female managers.

In Iran, women were prohibited from working in some occupations. Most women worked in the home, or for the family business, but usually did nothing for helping further economic development in the country. Iran can absolutely achieve economic growth through the addition and education of women to the workforce. Iran must continue to add more educated women to the workforce regardless of the initial investment, because the eventual return for doing so will be far greater.

Therefore, the present study investigates the change in lifestyle of women in Tonekabon city. More than 80 percent of women in Tonekabon are educated. They are much more exposed to means of mass communication. The procedure of modernization provides them with a vast array of new beliefs, values, behaviour, patterns and habits. They have to make new choices regarding dress, language they speak, and food they eat. The exposure is much more in urban society. Women are constantly faced with choices that often are in conflict with the traditional values and beliefs they have been brought up with. Therefore the researcher would like to study how these women change their lifestyle and how they spend their leisure time.

## XII. RESEARCH QUESTIONS

1. How do the women spend their leisure time in Tonekabon?
2. What is the recreation pattern and family recreation of the women in Tonekabon?
3. How do the women have access to information and mass media?
4. What are the personal habits of women in Tonekabon?

5. What are the socio-economic activities of women in Tonekabon?
6. Do the women in Tonekabon participate in political activities?
7. What are the women's attitudes towards their vital characteristics?
8. What is the nature of education and occupation among the women in Tonekabon?
9. What are the women's attitudes towards the social culture and religious ceremonies?
10. What are the women's attitude towards marriage ceremonies?

## XIII. SIGNIFICANCE OF THE STUDY

The process of modernization presents the members of the society a great many choices of new beliefs, values, behaviour patterns and habits to choose from. They have to make new choices regarding dress, the language they speak, and the food they eat, and those choices often result in social, cultural and emotional conflicts.

This study focuses on change in the lifestyle of urban women in Tonekabon city by understanding their attitudes towards all aspects of social, cultural, economic and political life.

This research discusses changes in women's lifestyle. Thus, aimed at contributing to society on the practical level, and to the field of urban anthropology at the theoretical level, it will add to the existing knowledge in the field.

## XIV. CHAPTER SCHEME

Chapter One presents the theoretical introduction of the thesis. Different concepts such as change in lifestyle, lifestyle and modernization, lifestyle and leisure time activities, lifestyle habits and the space, lifestyle and social classes and condition, lifestyle and management of body, lifestyle and mass media have been introduced. In addition to this is included the historical background of women in Iran, the statement of problem, significance of study and research questions and chapter scheme are introduced.

Chapter Two concerns with the research methodology applied in the present investigation. Ethnography of the city of Tonekabon, sample profile methodology of selection and collection and interpretation of data is discussed.

Chapter Three deals with lifestyle and leisure time activities, recreation pattern, access to information and mass media, and their personal habits. Moreover, in this chapter pictures of modern and traditional lifestyles are presented.

Chapter Four describes the socio-economic life and attitude toward education, attitude toward occupation and political participation.

Chapter Five discusses women's attitude toward these vital characterisliy, religious activities, customs and believes in the ceremonies.

Chapter Six highlights some of the major findings of the investigation and conclusions.

# 2

# Methodology

## I. THE SETTING

The present study is based on women in Tonekabon city. The city is located at the west part of Mazandaran and leads to Caspian Sea from North, to the North of Alborz Mountains from the South, to Chalkroud from the West and to Chaloos from the East. Tonekabon city is expanding about 1010 km located at the northern part of Islamic Republic of Iran. It is 252 km distant from the capital of Iran (Tehran) and 230 km to the capital of Mazandaran province. It is one of the seventeen cities in Mazandaran.

Tonekabon has two kinds of climates: 1. the north area where the weather is temperate and moderate. 2. The south area where the weather is cold. Lovely sight seeing made this city very attractive for the tourists and the local residents. The main attractive points are the Sayalan Height, Kokhsh Daran natural phenomenon, the beautiful sea side, Se Hezar hill area, Falak Deh mineral springs, Farhad Joy water fall, Daoya Sar plains, Danyal cave and Jal Dane garden which will be described separately. Cities affiliated to Tonekabon are as follow: Nashtarod, Abbas Abad, Salman Shahr and Kelar Abad.

In Tonekabon more than 99.72% of the population are Muslims and others are Zoroastrian and Christians. Also 83.42% of women in Tonekabon are literate. About 30% of women are students. The income of Tonekabon people is by working at industrial factories and manufacture, government jobs, doing business, private service, farming, agriculture, and so on.

## II. SELECTION OF AREA

Through the review, the researcher found that earlier researches were conducted in mainly urban areas as the impact of change of lifestyle was mostly in these places. Thus, before the selection of areas for study, the researcher visited the different localities of the Tonekabon city, such as Karim Abad township, Emam Khomeini street, Arian, Khobanrazgah, Golestan, Sabzehmeydan, Paskelayeh, Shohada township, Jomhory, Hafte Ter, Shirodi, Tonekabon Mohal, Golyjan, Azady Township areas. The researcher discussed questionnaires for the research with several informants, and then selected Aryan, Karim Abad Township, Shirodi Township, Khobanrazgah, Tonekabon Mohal, Golyjan, Sabzehmeydan, Paskelayeh, Shohada Township and Azady Township. Ten suburbs of Tonekabon city were selected for the present study. The selection of these areas was purposive. First, researcher selected these areas because people belonging to different socio-economic conditions stay there. Secondly, there are both educated and illiterate people in these areas. Thirdly, there were varieties of occupation in these areas.

## III. POPULATION UNDER STUDY AND SAMPLES

The population of Tonekabon is around 33,650, with 8,357 households (1995 census). Among them, 16,896 are women of which nearly 9,500 of women are between 16 to 65 years old. Out of these 9500 women, 5% sample was drawn for the present study. Consequently, 475 women of the households were selected from the areas such as Aryan, Karim Abad Township, Shirodi Township, Khobanrazgah, Tonekabon Mohal, Golyjan, Sabzehmeydan, Paskelayeh, Shohada Township and Azady Township. Using the techniques of simple random sampling.

## IV. INITIAL CONTACT AND RAPPORT ESTABLISHMENT

The Researcher, after finalizing the questionnaires and interviews under the supervision of her guide, went to Iran to distribute and collect the data. For distributing of questionnaire the researcher needed to take permission from different organization. First of all she has got a recommendation letter from the government of Tonekabon city. Then the researcher went to some related organizations to ask for their co-operation.

The researcher visited research areas several times, and spent time with potential respondents, and befriended many young university girls, who agreed to be respondents, and help with the research. The researcher spent time for explaining questions, interview informally, and visited with them some places like: coffee shop, park, sea shore, internet, library, Seshanbe (Tuesday) Bazaar and teach them how to contact with respondents and collect the questionnaire.

The researcher visited the areas under study twice or thrice a week and increased acquaintance with people under study, and informally discussed with them about the research problem and tried to get the cooperation from the interviewees before starting the actual fieldwork.

Moreover, the researcher arranged with them to take photos from their home, such as bedrooms, kitchen, sitting room, dining room and their home facilities. Details of their social life, the patterns of behaviour, the development and the expression of values and attitudes by involving the researcher in the daily life of the people were recorded. The researcher was also helped by Tonekabon Islamic Azad University, local government and government offices. Also, in distribution of questionnaire and collecting the data, some students and friends helped the researcher. Initially the researcher explained them how to distribute and collect data. Researcher distributed the questionnaire according to city map and area and census of Tonekabon city. While conducting the actual interviews, every question was explained to the interviewees by the researcher and then the questionnaire was filled out by the researcher herself. The questionnaire was kept with the respondents during the one or two days in some cases as they could not answer some questions immediately and required time for thinking. Some of the respondents were eager to give more information about the society. In some cases two or three sessions were required to complete the interview.

## V. METHOD OF DATA COLLECTION

Quantitative and qualitative data are often used together to complete and support assessment results. In-depth qualitative data is one of the features of an anthropological study. In the present study, a combination of qualitative and qualitative methods for data collection was used. The purpose of adopting a quantitative and qualitative combination was to develop the anthropological understanding of the community. These methods provided us a detailed description of the leisure time activities, modern and traditional lifestyle, behaviour, attitudes and opinion of the social group. Pelto (1972:11) said that "most contemporary mixing and interrelating of quantified material (from survey, official archives and other sources) with qualitative data, one gets from participant observation and informant's interviews... The qualitative and quantitative mix represents a significant point of departure for ensuring that re-studies of the same area at a later time, will have maximum comparability." In the present study, qualitative information was supplemented by participant and non-participant observation and in-depth unstructured interviews, as well as photography of lifestyle. Quantitative data were collected through questionnaires.

## VI. QUANTITATIVE DATA

### Pre-tests of the Questionnaire

A pilot study was conducted before the actual research. Researcher conducted a pilot study with Iranian women who are students in Pune, India. There fore the researcher found out the mistakes and inappropriate questions in the pilot study. The results were analyzed and written. After going to Iran, the researcher conducted a pilot study there also and sent the results to the guide in India. This helped the researcher to find out the unwanted mistakes and objectionable and inappropriate questions in questionnaire. Accordingly the researcher revised and modified the questionnaire and prepared the final draft of the questionnaire. The questionnaire consisted of 131 questions.

The questionnaire was divided into following eight sections:

1. General information of the respondents
2. Lifestyle/Leisure time activities
3. Recreation(visiting, family recreation, other activities, rest)
4. Personal Habits (food/nutrition, hygiene, house, sleep, work, clothes, smoking)
5. Access to information and Mass-media
6. Women's activities (social, economic, religion and political)
7. Attitude toward vital characteristics of women
8. Attitude toward education, occupation, values, customs and beliefs

Quantitative data is collected through the questionnaire and 475 questionnaires were filled.

## VII. QUALITATIVE DATA

The qualitative data were collected through thirty unstructured interviews of the elite of the Tonekabon community.

The elite from the community included business persons, clerks, teachers, physicians, engineers, lawyers, university teachers, government officers, housewives, and university students. The process of elite was done with the help of friends, students of university, and experienced persons. Unstructured interviews were of opened type. There was much freedom for the interviewees to express their views freely and frankly. The respondents had willingly spared their time and talked freely and in an elaborate manner. The interviews were conducted according to the convenience of the informants. At the time of the interview, the respondents were encouraged to talk about the subject clearly. In some cases, the informants preferred to give answers in writing in addition to speaking. Each unstructured interview was completed in several sessions.

## VIII. DATA PROCESSING

The data collected through the questionnaire were processed in a systematic way, as follows:

### Editing

The questionnaire was edited, for checking their completeness and accuracy. This was because, in spite of the researcher's experience and knowledge, certain errors, gaps, inconsistencies remained in the schedules. To avoid all these problems, careful editing of the questionnaire was carried out.

### Coding

All data present in the questionnaire were converted into a numerical form and presented on the coding matrix. A coding frame was prepared for each question.

### Analysis

The data contained in the questionnaire were analyzed by using the Statistical Packages of Social Sciences (SPSS).The qualitative data analysed mutuality.

## IX. THE SAMPLE PROFILES

### Age

The above data given, presents the age composition of the samples under study. It is found from respondents belonging to different age groups ranging from 16 years to above 55 years. (34.2%) of the respondents belong to the 16-24 years age group; (21.9%) belong to 25-35 years age group; (29.2%) belong to the 35-44 years age group; and (14.5%) belong to the 45-54 years age group and less (2%) belong to the age group of 55 years above. It is evident that highest percentages of the respondents were young.

## Marital Status

As regard to marital status of the respondents, (59.8%) were married and (34.2%) unmarried. Very few (3.1%) of the respondents were widows, and ( 2.9%) divorcees.

## Birth Location

Nearly three-fourth (70%) of the respondents were born in the city and one- third (30%) of the respondents were born in villages.

## Number of Children

Answering the question regarding the number of children, (40.8%) of the respondents said that they have one daughter only, and (35.7%) had one son only. (9.7%) of them had two daughters and few (8.4%) answered two sons. (3.4%) of the respondents had one daughter and one son, (1.7%) said three children and at last very few (1%) stated that they have more than four children.

## Length of Residence in Tonekabon

Half of the respondents (50.3%) have been born in Tonekabon city. (13.4%) of them were staying in the city for 1-5 years 5-10 years ago. (11.2%) said from they have been living there. around (9.8%) of the respondents used to live in that city since 10-15 years. Nearly (15.3%) were living in Tonekabon for more than 15 years.

## Family Type

In the classification of the respondents on the basis of the type of the families they live in, It was found from the study that (82.9%) of the respondents were living in joint families. And only (17.1%) of the respondents were living in nucleas families. It means that a higher percentage lived in joint families.

## Types of the Houses they are Residing In

The present study shows that half (55.6%) of the respondents lived in flats and above (44.4%) of the respondents have bungalow houses.

## House Rented or Own

In this study as many as (73.5%) of the respondents said that, they have rented a house and nearly (26.5%) of the respondents stated that they have their own houses.

## Education Status

As far as formal education was concerned, more than a half (52.8%) were graduates and above; (25.9%) had high school diploma; (11.3%) studied up to primary school; (6.8%) secondary school and very few (3.2%) were illiterate.

## Occupation Status

Nearly (18.9%) of the respondents were unemployed and (23.2%) were self employed, clerk, business women. Also (10.1%) were students and nearly (29.6%) were teachers, principles, government officers and (18.2%) of the respondents were doctors, engineers, lawyers, and professors.

## Income

There were around (32.7%) of the women respondents whose monthly income was zero because they were house when. And nearly (12.3%) of them had monthly income below one million Rails (one million Rails = five thousand rupees). Around (24.8%) of them had monthly income ranging between one to three million Rails. Above (11.6%) of the respondents had monthly income between three to six million Rails. Also, about (18.6%) of the respondents had six million

Rails and above monthly income. Therefore in this study they have respondents from the lower strata to the higher strata in terms of monthly income.

## Religion

In the present study, the majority (94.4%) of the respondents were Muslim, around (2.9%) Zoroastrian, nearly (1.3%) Christian, and nearly (1.3%) of the respondents were from other religions.

# 3

# Lifestyle and Leisure Time Activity

This chapter focuses on the lifestyle of the women of Tonekabon city in Iran. To understand the lifestyle of the urban women in Iran, different parameters such as, their leisure time activities, recreation patterns, personal habits, access to information and mass-media were studied.

The concept of lifestyle has a long history in numerous disciplines and fields of study, containing leisure studies. The term 'lifestyle' first appeared in 1939. Alvin Toffler predicted an explosion of lifestyles (sub-cults) as diversity increases in post-industrial societies. Pre-modern societies did not require a term approaching sub-culture or 'lifestyle', as different ways of living were expressed as entirely different cultures, religions, ethnicities or by an oppressed minority racial group. As such, the minority culture was always seen as alien or other. 'Lifestyles', by comparison, are accepted or partially accepted differences within the majority culture or group. This tolerance of differentiation within a majority culture seems to be associated with modernity and capitalism. Anthony J. Veal (2001) points out that a large feature of the history of leisure studies have been the inquiry to define diversities in patterns of leisure participation between individuals and groups of individuals. Larrabee and Meyrsohn (1961) attribute the meaning of leisure to vary between state of freedom with various activities and a state of contemplation.

When people speak and write about 'leisure' they often use the word to mean different things. Therefore we shall look first at various definitions of leisure and related concepts such as free time, play and recreation. In order to put our modern ideas and experiences of leisure into wider context, we shall then examine what leisure means to people in simpler, non-industrial societies.

S. R Parker (1976: 17) says that, there are three broad ways of defining leisure.

First definition, given by H. P. Fairchild (1944), is to take the twenty-four hours in the day and subtract from them periods which are not leisure: working, sleeping, eating, and attending to physiological need, and so on. Other possible things to take out of total time to leave only leisure include travelling to and preparing for work, meeting obligations toward others, and working around the home. In the dictionary of sociology: leisure is 'time devoted to work, and other necessities, subtracted from twenty-four – which gives the surplus time'.

The second definition is apparently preferred by several sociologists in that it is not a period of time but qualitative activity of a person. This would fit the more modern image, where it is the type of activities such as those discussed in this chapter. This definition was given in (1974) by A. Touraine. When referred to, it is frequently used with the quality of freedom, a necessary criterion for leisure. The third definition seeks to combine both freedom and activity, but it emphasizes freedom from rules and imposed models of behaviour. Ultimately, the definition preferred normally for leisure is as follows:

> 'the time which an individual has free from work or other duties and which may be utilized for purpose of relaxation, diversion, social achievement, or personal development'.

The Wikipedia Dictionary agrees with this definition by stating that leisure is time away from cares and troubles in non-compulsory activities such as employment in work, household duties, stressful daily activity, running businesses, and education and even from eating and sleeping. In a sense, it accords with the first definition as well. It is referred to [in

American English] as 'free time'. We note that there is no strict distinction between compulsory activity and leisure as some compulsory activities may be done for pleasure.

Jain Brothers (1984: 183) in his study, 'The Idea that Women Work, or do not Work", stated that it freed from long hours of work or non working are different leisure time activities. Today a question arises in the context of the countries where a social-welfare system has emerged bringing with it somewhat reduced work-day, what, in fact, are the workers doing during leisure? Do they try to develop aesthetic interest? Or, do they not? And if not? Why not? The extents to which any segment of a society's population participates in civic activities, and belongs to one or the other organization are means through which individuals cope with their environment.'

Gordon Dahl (1972:21) writes: "today's people need for leisure is not free time only but a free spirit; not more hobbies or amusements but a sense of grace and peace which will lift us beyond our busy schedules."

Max Kaplan, one of America's foremost scholars on the topic, suggested in 1960 that any (specific) thing can become a base for leisure. This includes an antithesis to work, fewer social obligations, an understanding of freedom, setting a range from inconsequence to importance, etc. Kaplan has suggested six categories of leisure activities.

The French sociologist Joffre Dumazedier (1967) believes that leisure serves three main functions to the individual: 'relaxation, diversion, or broadening his knowledge and his spontaneous social participation.'

In (1961), Edward Gross added certain functions to a social group, such as a friendly drink with work colleagues and sports, even national identification.

Also Robert Havighurst (1957) concluded from his studies that different age, sex and social class groups can derive similar values from their leisure, even though its content is different.

Ray Maw and others in the Multi-National Time Budget Research Project, have also given the classifying types of leisure activities.

**Table 3.1 : Kaplan's Classifying Types of Leisure Activities**

| *Kaplan* | *Maw* | *Time Budget* |
|---|---|---|
| Sociability | Talking, Parties, etc. | Social life, Conversation, |
| Association | | Organizations |
| Game | Sport and Active Play | Sports |
| Art | Theatre | Movies, Theatre, etc. |
| Movement | Dining and Drinking, out, Do it Yourself, Gardening, driving for Pleasure | Walking |
| Immobility | Relaxing, Passive Play, T.V. Radio, Reading, etc. | Resting |
| | Hobbies | T.V. Radio and Reading |

Another way of approaching the classification of leisure experiences is in terms of functions that they serve for individuals. Joffre Dumazedier (1972) does this by distinguishing three functions, those of relaxation, diversion, and developing of the personality.

Rolf Meyersohn (1972) arrives at an expanded version of these functions by taking into account certain issues which face individuals, as well as:

(1) It is necessary for all of us to have intervals between bouts of work and other obligatory activities-hence leisure as rest, recuperation.

(2) We have a need for diversion, to gain pleasure from spectacles and performances of various kinds-leisure as entertainment.

(3) Nevertheless, the dominant values in our society encourage us to seek achievement in all spheres of life and to be competent in what we do- leisure as self-realization.

(4) Finally (as if to question the material basis of many

meaning attached to the term 'leisure') we may feel the need for spiritual renewal, difficult though this concept is to define and measure Sage Foundation. Therefore in the present study in order to get a broad picture of how women spend their leisure time, Kaplan's six categories of the leisure activity such as: Sociability, association, game, art, movement, immobility have been studied. The respondents were asked a range of questions about the amount of time they spend doing leisure activities such as: gym, body building, clubs, cinema, public library, festivals, museum, concert hall, exhibition, park, historical places, tourist place, voyage, hobbies, restaurant, fast food restaurants, coffee shops, social work.

**Table 3.2 : Leisure Time Activities**

| *Leisure time activities* | *Usually* | | *Some Time* | | *Often* | | *Never* | | *Total* |
|---|---|---|---|---|---|---|---|---|---|
| | *Freq.* | *%* | *Freq.* | *%* | *Freq.* | *%* | *Freq.* | *%* | |
| Gym | 146 | 36.1 | 110 | 27.2 | 9 | 2.2 | 139 | 34.4 | 404 |
| Body building clubs | 43 | 11.7 | 107 | 29.2 | 11 | 3.0 | 206 | 56.1 | 367 |
| Cinema | 34 | 9.1 | 165 | 44.2 | 12 | 3.2 | 162 | 43.4 | 373 |
| Public library | 53 | 14.1 | 168 | 44.8 | 19 | 5.1 | 135 | 36.0 | 375 |
| Festival | 39 | 10.9 | 114 | 31.9 | 13 | 3.6 | 191 | 53.5 | 357 |
| Museum | 28 | 7.8 | 112 | 31.1 | 12 | 3.3 | 208 | 57.8 | 360 |
| Concert hall | 22 | 6.5 | 85 | 25.0 | 26 | 7.6 | 207 | 60.9 | 340 |
| Exhibition | 36 | 10.4 | 138 | 39.9 | 55 | 15.9 | 117 | 33.8 | 346 |
| Park | 64 | 16.8 | 164 | 42.9 | 88 | 23.0 | 66 | 17.3 | 382 |
| Historical places | 44 | 12.5 | 126 | 35.8 | 56 | 15.9 | 126 | 35.8 | 352 |
| Tourist place | 44 | 12.6 | 119 | 34.2 | 53 | 15.2 | 132 | 37.9 | 348 |
| Voyage hobbies | 23 | 7.1 | 47 | 14.5 | 32 | 9.9 | 222 | 68.5 | 324 |
| Restaurant | 35 | 10.1 | 116 | 33.3 | 66 | 19.0 | 131 | 37.6 | 348 |
| Fast food restaurant | 52 | 14.4 | 147 | 40.8 | 71 | 19.7 | 90 | 25.0 | 360 |
| Coffee shops | 39 | 11.4 | 119 | 34.8 | 63 | 18.4 | 121 | 35.4 | 342 |
| Social work | 53 | 15.0 | 126 | 35.7 | 81 | 22.9 | 93 | 26.3 | 353 |

In the present investigation (Table 3.2), all respondents have their own leisure time activities. The above table shows that, nearly 83.7% respondents said that they go to a park, and more than 72% tend to go for social work, fast food restaurant, and exhibition; more than 63% replied they like to go gym, historical place, tourist place, restaurant, coffee shop; and above 56.6% go to cinema; over 43% answered public library, body-building clubs; and higher than 39.1% concert hall and 21.5% respondents indulge in festivals, museums, voyage hobbies.

It is clear from the above discussion that most of the women spend their leisure time according to traditional pattern of spending as well on modern time such as; visiting the parks, public library, celebrating festivals, museum, historical places, and social work fradifional. Gym, body building clubs, cinema, museum, concert hall, exhibition, tourist place, voyage, hobbies, restaurant, fast food restaurant, coffee shops and social work modern. Most young respondents clearly spend lots of time in modern pattern of leisure time activities. So we can observe both traditional and modern pattern of spending leisure time. Thus, one can say that there is change in the lifestyle as long as leisure time activities are concerned and also there is continuity to some respect.

The researcher has done a detailed study of some families to find out the leisure time activities of women in Tonekabon city.

1. One lady named Mrs Rostampour, staying at Shirud, was 38 years old. She had two daughtered, and one son. She believed that her leisure time depends on the situations which come up in life. For instance, one of her daughters was a pupil at a primary school and she liked to go to parks, to go outside with her mother; the other one was going to college in another city and when she came back home, she spendt her time with friends, or going to parties, libraries and so on. Her son was a student of computer engineering. He also usually spent his leisure time by working on the computer,

chatting, reading sport magazine, etc. Thus, Mrs Rostampour had to adapt herself to her children and how they liked to spent their leisure time. She was an employee at a university and her husband was an engineer. She had to work every day from morning 8:00 till the afternoon at 2:30. During the New Year and summer holidays, they always planued to travel with their children. Also some time going to fast food restaurants with the family.

2. Another lady, named Mrs. Marjan, who is the supervisor of kindergarten, is 30 years old. She lived in the Arian area. She had two daughters; one of them was 2 years and the other one was 12 years. Her husband was a business man. She said, at weekends, she spent her leisure time with her mother's family and some times with her in law's family. Also some times, Mrs. Marjan went for picnics which was planned by the kindergarten. During the New Year's holiday she and her family went for a vacation to tourist places.

3. In Mrs. Samimi's family there was a son and one daughter. She lived in the Azadi area. Mrs. Samimi and her husband were engineers. Her daughter was a student of medicine and her son a student of engineering. She liked to spend her leisure time by doing the housework, decorating the house and using the computer by chatting and getting information from the internet. She always planed how to spend her leisure time because she always put her family first; so, she not want to sacrifice her family because of her hobbies. Since her husband was very busy, she always tried to make a peaceful atmosphere at home. Mrs. Samimi wanted her husband to have peace, and rest quietly when he came home. She was not the type to unnecessarily spendt her time by going out to a neighbour, etc. Her daughter studied hard and she came home once a month so they spent their time together when the daughter was at home. Similarly her son also came home once a month and they spent their time with each other.

4. In Mrs. Ghobadie's family, there were four daughters and two sons. She was 52 years old and a house wife. Her

husband was a farmer. Her hobbies are watching TV and listening to radio. She also spent her time by watching the flowers in the garden or by helping her husband. All her children well married and all of them worked. They lived in different cities and during the holidays they came to their parents' home. When Mrs. Ghobadi visited them in their houses, she spent her time with her grandchildren; for example, she took them to parks. Sometimes she went to religious cities to pray.

It is clear from the case study that the respondents spent their leisure time in a traditional way such as; going to parks, doing social work, going out to a neighbour, going to religious cities, watching TV and listening to radio, visiting mother's family and some times in-law's family. And also spent leisure time in modern pattern such as; going to fast food restaurants, visiting exhibitions, tourist places, and chatting.

Nasser Fakouhi, and Fereshte Ansari, (2002) in their study *'Leisure Time and Cultural Personality Formation in Two Girls' High Schools in the City of Tehran'* found that girls from the modern, rich higher school level families spent their leisure time watching satellite T.V. channels, dating in coffee houses, going to night parties, trying modern art forms such as playing musical instruments, painting, skiing and so on. But those from the 'traditional' families would usually spend their leisure time praying in the mosque, being a member of a religious group or sewing and weaving carpets.

Narges Abedinizadeh, (1993) in her survey 'How Higher School Girls in 17$^{th}$ area of Tehran Spend Their Leisure Time', stated that the school girls' leisure time is to a great extent dependent on the father's job and the family income.

Farzane Zalnejad, (1991) in his study regarding leisure time, 'How 11$^{th}$ Standard School Girls in 17$^{th}$ and third area of Tehran Spend Their Leisure Time', believes that spending leisure time is so much dependent on the lifestyle. For instance, girls spend their leisure time, mostly, helping their mother

Table 3.3: Age and Leisure Time Activities

| | | *16-24* | | *25-34* | | *35-44* | | *45-54* | | *55 above* | | *Total* |
|---|---|---|---|---|---|---|---|---|---|---|---|---|
| | | *Freq.* | % | *Freq.* | % | *Freq.* | % | *Freq.* | % | *Freq.* | % | |
| 1 | 2 | 3 | 4 | 5 | 6 | 7 | 8 | 9 | 10 | 11 | 12 | 13 |
| Gym | often | 55 | 38.7 | 30 | 21.1 | 44 | 31.0 | 12 | 8.5 | 1 | .7 | **142** |
| | some time | 33 | 30.6 | 29 | 26.9 | 31 | 28.7 | 15 | 13.9 | 0 | .0 | **108** |
| | mostly | 3 | 33.3 | 3 | 33.3 | 2 | 22.2 | 1 | 11.1 | 0 | .0 | **9** |
| | never | 51 | 37.8 | 23 | 17.0 | 32 | 23.7 | 29 | 21.5 | 0 | .0 | **135** |
| | **Total** | **142** | **36.0** | **85** | **21.6** | **109** | **27.7** | **57** | **14.5** | **1** | **.3** | **394** |
| Body building clubs | often | 11 | 27.5 | 7 | 17.5 | 17 | 42.5 | 5 | 12.5 | 0 | .0 | **40** |
| | some time | 30 | 28.3 | 29 | 27.4 | 38 | 35.8 | 9 | 8.5 | 0 | .0 | **106** |
| | mostly | 6 | 60.0 | 3 | 30.0 | 1 | 10.0 | 0 | .0 | 0 | .0 | **10** |
| | never | 89 | 44.1 | 34 | 16.8 | 42 | 20.8 | 36 | 17.8 | 1 | .5 | **202** |
| | **Total** | **136** | **38.0** | **73** | **20.4** | **98** | **27.4** | **50** | **14.0** | **1** | **.3** | **358** |
| Cinema | often | 13 | 41.9 | 4 | 12.9 | 12 | 38.7 | 2 | 6.5 | 0 | .0 | **31** |
| | some time | 68 | 41.7 | 37 | 22.7 | 42 | 25.8 | 16 | 9.8 | 0 | .0 | **163** |
| | mostly | 9 | 75.0 | 1 | 8.3 | 2 | 16.7 | 0 | .0 | 0 | .0 | **12** |
| | never | 51 | 32.3 | 29 | 18.4 | 42 | 26.6 | 35 | 22.2 | 1 | .6 | **158** |
| | **Total** | **141** | **38.7** | **71** | **19.5** | **98** | **26.9** | **53** | **14.6** | **1** | **.3** | **364** |

**(Contd.)**

| 1 | 2 | 3 | 4 | 5 | 6 | 7 | 8 | 9 | 10 | 11 | 12 | 13 |
|---|---|---|---|---|---|---|---|---|---|---|---|---|
| Public library | often | 30 | 57.7 | 6 | 11.5 | 13 | 25.0 | 3 | 5.8 | 0 | .0 | **52** |
| | some time | 75 | 45.5 | 38 | 23.0 | 36 | 21.8 | 16 | 9.7 | 0 | .0 | **165** |
| | often | 8 | 42.1 | 5 | 26.3 | 4 | 21.1 | 2 | 10.5 | 0 | .0 | **19** |
| | never | 30 | 22.7 | 25 | 18.9 | 44 | 33.3 | 32 | 24.2 | 1 | .8 | **132** |
| | **Total** | **143** | **38.9** | **74** | **20.1** | **97** | **26.4** | **53** | **14.4** | **1** | **.3** | **368** |
| Festival | often | 19 | 50.0 | 5 | 13.2 | 11 | 28.9 | 3 | 7.9 | 0 | .0 | **38** |
| | some time | 47 | 41.6 | 22 | 19.5 | 34 | 30.1 | 10 | 8.8 | 0 | .0 | **113** |
| | mostly | 5 | 38.5 | 2 | 15.4 | 4 | 30.8 | 2 | 15.4 | 0 | .0 | **13** |
| | never | 61 | 33.0 | 39 | 21.1 | 49 | 26.5 | 35 | 18.9 | 1 | .5 | **185** |
| | **Total** | **132** | **37.8** | **68** | **19.5** | **98** | **28.1** | **50** | **14.3** | **1** | **.3** | **349** |
| Museum | often | 16 | 57.1 | 1 | 3.6 | 9 | 32.1 | 2 | 7.1 | 0 | .0 | **28** |
| | sometime | 36 | 32.4 | 25 | 22.5 | 35 | 31.5 | 15 | 13.5 | 0 | .0 | **111** |
| | mostly | 4 | 33.3 | 3 | 25.0 | 4 | 33.3 | 1 | 8.3 | 0 | .0 | **12** |
| | never | 80 | 39.6 | 39 | 19.3 | 49 | 24.3 | 33 | 16.3 | 1 | .5 | **202** |
| | **Total** | **136** | **38.5** | **68** | **19.3** | **97** | **27.5** | **51** | **14.4** | **1** | **.3** | **353** |

**(Contd.)**

| 1 | 2 | 3 | 4 | 5 | 6 | 7 | 8 | 9 | 10 | 11 | 12 | 13 |
|---|---|---|---|---|---|---|---|---|---|---|---|---|
| Concert hall | often | 13 | 61.9 | 3 | 14.3 | 2 | 9.5 | 2 | 9.5 | 1 | 4.8 | **21** |
| | some time | 34 | 41.0 | 21 | 25.3 | 22 | 26.5 | 6 | 7.2 | 0 | .0 | **83** |
| | mostly | 7 | 26.9 | 5 | 19.2 | 9 | 34.6 | 5 | 19.2 | 0 | .0 | **26** |
| | never | 81 | 39.7 | 35 | 17.2 | 53 | 26.0 | 35 | 17.2 | 0 | .0 | **204** |
| | **Total** | **135** | **40.4** | **64** | **19.2** | **86** | **25.7** | **48** | **14.4** | **1** | **.3** | **334** |
| Exhibition | often | 17 | 47.2 | 9 | 25.0 | 9 | 25.0 | 1 | 2.8 | 0 | .0 | **36** |
| | sometime | 55 | 40.4 | 41 | 30.1 | 28 | 20.6 | 12 | 8.8 | 0 | .0 | **136** |
| | mostly | 23 | 41.8 | 7 | 12.7 | 17 | 30.9 | 8 | 14.5 | 0 | .0 | **55** |
| | never | 35 | 30.7 | 17 | 14.9 | 33 | 28.9 | 28 | 24.6 | 1 | .9 | **114** |
| | **Total** | **130** | **38.1** | **74** | **21.7** | **87** | **25.5** | **49** | **14.4** | **1** | **.3** | **341** |
| Park | often | 22 | 36.1 | 22 | 36.1 | 15 | 24.6 | 2 | 3.3 | 0 | .0 | **61** |
| | some time | 62 | 38.3 | 41 | 25.3 | 45 | 27.8 | 14 | 8.6 | 0 | .0 | **162** |
| | mostly | 39 | 44.3 | 19 | 21.6 | 19 | 21.6 | 11 | 12.5 | 0 | .0 | **88** |
| | never | 16 | 25.0 | 4 | 6.3 | 18 | 28.1 | 25 | 39.1 | 1 | 1.6 | **64** |
| | **Total** | **139** | **37.1** | **86** | **22.9** | **97** | **25.9** | **52** | **13.9** | **1** | **.3** | **375** |
| Historical places | often | 15 | 34.9 | 9 | 20.9 | 15 | 34.9 | 4 | 9.3 | 0 | .0 | **43** |
| | sometime | 51 | 40.5 | 32 | 25.4 | 32 | 25.4 | 11 | 8.7 | 0 | .0 | **126** |
| | mostly | 20 | 35.7 | 9 | 16.1 | 18 | 32.1 | 9 | 16.1 | 0 | .0 | **56** |
| | never | 48 | 39.3 | 19 | 15.6 | 28 | 23.0 | 27 | 22.1 | 0 | .0 | **122** |
| | **Total** | **134** | **38.6** | **69** | **19.9** | **93** | **26.8** | **51** | **14.7** | 0 | .0 | **347** |

**(Contd.)**

| 1 | 2 | 3 | 4 | 5 | 6 | 7 | 8 | 9 | 10 | 11 | 12 | 13 |
|---|---|---|---|---|---|---|---|---|---|---|---|---|
| Tourist place | often | 21 | 51.2 | 6 | 14.6 | 10 | 24.4 | 4 | 9.8 | 0 | .0 | **41** |
| | some time | 44 | 37.6 | 31 | 26.5 | 32 | 27.4 | 9 | 7.7 | 1 | .9 | **117** |
| | mostly | 21 | 39.6 | 12 | 22.6 | 15 | 28.3 | 5 | 9.4 | 0 | .0 | **53** |
| | never | 46 | 35.7 | 19 | 14.7 | 34 | 26.4 | 30 | 23.3 | 0 | .0 | **129** |
| | **Total** | **132** | **38.8** | **68** | **20.0** | **91** | **26.8** | **48** | **14.1** | **1** | **.3** | **340** |
| Voyage hobbies | often | 14 | 66.7 | 3 | 14.3 | 4 | 19.0 | 0 | .0 | 0 | .0 | **21** |
| | some time | 16 | 34.0 | 13 | 27.7 | 13 | 27.7 | 4 | 8.5 | 1 | 2.1 | **47** |
| | mostly | 14 | 43.8 | 5 | 15.6 | 10 | 31.3 | 3 | 9.4 | 0 | .0 | **32** |
| | never | 80 | 36.7 | 43 | 19.7 | 56 | 25.7 | 39 | 17.9 | 0 | .0 | **218** |
| | **Total** | **124** | **39.0** | **64** | **20.1** | **83** | **26.1** | **46** | **14.5** | **1** | **.3** | **318** |
| Restaurant | often | 12 | 36.4 | 9 | 27.3 | 10 | 30.3 | 2 | 6.1 | 0 | .0 | **33** |
| | some time | 47 | 42.0 | 27 | 24.1 | 30 | 26.8 | 8 | 7.1 | 0 | .0 | **112** |
| | mostly | 25 | 37.9 | 11 | 16.7 | 19 | 28.8 | 11 | 16.7 | 0 | .0 | **66** |
| | never | 50 | 38.5 | 20 | 15.4 | 30 | 23.1 | 29 | 22.3 | 1 | .8 | **130** |
| | **Total** | **134** | **39.3** | **67** | **19.6** | **89** | **26.1** | **50** | **14.7** | **1** | **.3** | **341** |
| Fast food restaurant | often | 22 | 43.1 | 16 | 31.4 | 10 | 19.6 | 3 | 5.9 | 0 | .0 | **51** |
| | some time | 64 | 44.4 | 31 | 21.5 | 33 | 22.9 | 15 | 10.4 | 1 | .7 | **144** |
| | mostly | 30 | 42.9 | 11 | 15.7 | 20 | 28.6 | 9 | 12.9 | 0 | .0 | **70** |
| | never | 22 | 25.0 | 15 | 17.0 | 25 | 28.4 | 26 | 29.5 | 0 | .0 | **88** |
| | **Total** | **138** | **39.1** | **73** | **20.7** | **88** | **24.9** | **53** | **15.0** | **1** | **.3** | **353** |

(Contd.)

| 1 | 2 | 3 | 4 | 5 | 6 | 7 | 8 | 9 | 10 | 11 | 12 | 13 |
|---|---|---|---|---|---|---|---|---|---|---|---|---|
| Coffee-shops | often | 21 | 56.8 | 4 | 10.8 | 10 | 27.0 | 2 | 5.4 | 0 | .0 | **37** |
| | some time | 51 | 44.0 | 36 | 31.0 | 24 | 20.7 | 5 | 4.3 | 0 | .0 | **116** |
| | mostly | 28 | 44.4 | 8 | 12.7 | 19 | 30.2 | 7 | 11.1 | 1 | 1.6 | **63** |
| | never | 33 | 27.7 | 18 | 15.1 | 36 | 30.3 | 32 | 26.9 | 0 | .0 | **119** |
| | **Total** | **133** | **39.7** | **66** | **19.7** | **89** | **26.6** | **46** | **13.7** | **1** | **.3** | **335** |
| Social work | often | 23 | 44.2 | 10 | 19.2 | 18 | 34.6 | 1 | 1.9 | 0 | .0 | **52** |
| | some time | 54 | 43.5 | 33 | 26.6 | 26 | 21.0 | 11 | 8.9 | 0 | .0 | **124** |
| | mostly | 33 | 41.3 | 14 | 17.5 | 24 | 30.0 | 8 | 10.0 | 1 | 1.3 | **80** |
| | never | 24 | 26.4 | 9 | 9.9 | 28 | 30.8 | 30 | 33.0 | 0 | .0 | **91** |
| | **Total** | **134** | **38.6** | **66** | **19.0** | **96** | **27.7** | **50** | **14.4** | **1** | **.3** | **347** |
| Any other | often | 12 | 37.5 | 13 | 40.6 | 5 | 15.6 | 2 | 6.3 | 0 | .0 | **32** |
| | some time | 29 | 45.3 | 19 | 29.7 | 11 | 17.2 | 5 | 7.8 | 0 | .0 | **64** |
| | mostly | 14 | 41.2 | 5 | 14.7 | 13 | 38.2 | 1 | 2.9 | 1 | 2.9 | **34** |
| | never | 14 | 26.9 | 6 | 11.5 | 12 | 23.1 | 20 | 38.5 | 0 | .0 | **52** |
| | **Total** | **69** | **37.9** | **43** | **23.6** | **41** | **22.5** | **28** | **15.4** | **1** | **.5** | **182** |

**(Contd.)**

Table 3.4: Marital Status and Leisure Time Activities

| *Activities* | | *Unmarried* | | *Married* | | *Divorce* | | *Widow* | | *Total* |
|---|---|---|---|---|---|---|---|---|---|---|
| | | *Freq.* | % | *Freq.* | % | *Freq.* | % | *Freq.* | % | |
| 1 | 2 | 3 | 4 | 5 | 6 | 7 | 8 | 9 | 10 | 11 |
| Gym | Often | 52 | 36.6 | 83 | 58.5 | 7 | 4.9 | 0 | .0 | 142 |
| | some time | 37 | 35.6 | 63 | 60.6 | 2 | 1.9 | 2 | 1.9 | 104 |
| | mostly | 2 | 22.2 | 7 | 77.8 | 0 | .0 | 0 | .0 | 9 |
| | never | 47 | 36.4 | 68 | 52.7 | 4 | 3.1 | 10 | 7.8 | 129 |
| | Total | **138** | **35.9** | **221** | **57.6** | **13** | **3.4** | **12** | **3.1** | **384** |
| Body building clubs | often | 11 | 26.8 | 26 | 63.4 | 3 | 7.3 | 1 | 2.4 | 41 |
| | some time | 29 | 29.0 | 68 | 68.0 | 2 | 2.0 | 1 | 1.0 | 100 |
| | mostly | 7 | 70.0 | 3 | 30.0 | 0 | .0 | 0 | .0 | 10 |
| | never | 85 | 42.5 | 99 | 49.5 | 6 | 3.0 | 10 | 5.0 | 200 |
| | Total | **132** | **37.6** | **196** | **55.8** | **11** | **3.1** | **12** | **3.4** | **351** |
| Cinema | often | 14 | 42.4 | 16 | 48.5 | 2 | 6.1 | 1 | 3.0 | 33 |
| | some time | 59 | 37.8 | 90 | 57.7 | 3 | 1.9 | 4 | 2.6 | 156 |
| | mostly | 8 | 88.9 | 1 | 11.1 | 0 | .0 | 0 | .0 | 9 |
| | never | 52 | 32.7 | 92 | 57.9 | 7 | 4.4 | 8 | 5.0 | 159 |
| | Total | **133** | **37.3** | **199** | **55.7** | **12** | **3.4** | **13** | **3.6** | **357** |

(Contd.)

| 1 | 2 | 3 | 4 | 5 | 6 | 7 | 8 | 9 | 10 | 11 |
|---|---|---|---|---|---|---|---|---|---|---|
| Public Library | often | 28 | 53.8 | 23 | 44.2 | 1 | 1.9 | 0 | .0 | 52 |
| | some time | 74 | 46.0 | 80 | 49.7 | 3 | 1.9 | 4 | 2.5 | 161 |
| | often | 9 | 50.0 | 7 | 38.9 | 0 | .0 | 2 | 11.1 | 18 |
| | never | 30 | 23.8 | 84 | 66.7 | 7 | 5.6 | 5 | 4.0 | 126 |
| | **Total** | **141** | **39.5** | **194** | **54.3** | **11** | **3.1** | **11** | **3.1** | **357** |
| Festival | often | 19 | 50.0 | 18 | 47.4 | 1 | 2.6 | 0 | .0 | 38 |
| | some time | 43 | 38.7 | 62 | 55.9 | 2 | 1.8 | 4 | 3.6 | 111 |
| | mostly | 6 | 46.2 | 6 | 46.2 | 0 | .0 | 1 | 7.7 | 13 |
| | never | 62 | 34.8 | 101 | 56.7 | 8 | 4.5 | 7 | 3.9 | 178 |
| | **Total** | **130** | **38.2** | **187** | **55.0** | **11** | **3.2** | **12** | **3.5** | **340** |
| Museum | often | 14 | 53.8 | 11 | 42.3 | 1 | 3.8 | 0 | .0 | 26 |
| | sometime | 35 | 32.1 | 65 | 59.6 | 3 | 2.8 | 6 | 5.5 | 109 |
| | mostly | 5 | 41.7 | 6 | 50.0 | 0 | .0 | 1 | 8.3 | 12 |
| | never | 79 | 40.3 | 105 | 53.6 | 7 | 3.6 | 5 | 2.6 | 196 |
| | **Total** | **133** | **38.8** | **187** | **54.5** | **11** | **3.2** | **12** | **3.5** | **343** |
| Concert hall | often | 10 | 50.0 | 9 | 45.0 | 1 | 5.0 | 0 | .0 | 20 |
| | some time | 32 | 39.0 | 48 | 58.5 | 2 | 2.4 | 0 | .0 | 82 |
| | mostly | 8 | 34.8 | 13 | 56.5 | 0 | .0 | 2 | 8.7 | 23 |

(Contd.)

| 1 | 2 | 3 | 4 | 5 | 6 | 7 | 8 | 9 | 10 | 11 |
|---|---|---|---|---|---|---|---|---|---|---|
| | never | 79 | 40.3 | 102 | 52.0 | 7 | 3.6 | 8 | 4.1 | 196 |
| | **Total** | **129** | **40.2** | **172** | **53.6** | 10 | **3.1** | 10 | **3.1** | **321** |
| Exhibition | often | 16 | 50.0 | 15 | 46.9 | 1 | 3.1 | 0 | .0 | 32 |
| | sometime | 55 | 43.0 | 70 | 54.7 | 1 | .8 | 2 | 1.6 | 128 |
| | mostly | 25 | 49.0 | 19 | 37.3 | 2 | 3.9 | 5 | 9.8 | 51 |
| | never | 34 | 29.6 | 72 | 62.6 | 5 | 4.3 | 4 | 3.5 | 115 |
| | **Total** | **130** | **39.9** | **176** | **54.0** | 9 | **2.8** | 11 | **3.4** | **326** |
| Park | often | 19 | 32.8 | 36 | 62.1 | 3 | 5.2 | 0 | .0 | 58 |
| | some time | 58 | 36.9 | 94 | 59.9 | 2 | 1.3 | 3 | 1.9 | 157 |
| | mostly | 41 | 49.4 | 36 | 43.4 | 2 | 2.4 | 4 | 4.8 | 83 |
| | never | 15 | 23.1 | 42 | 64.6 | 4 | 6.2 | 4 | 6.2 | 65 |
| | **Total** | **133** | **36.6** | **208** | **57.3** | 11 | **3.0** | 11 | **3.0** | **363** |
| Historical places | often | 13 | 31.7 | 27 | 65.9 | 1 | 2.4 | 0 | .0 | 41 |
| | sometime | 48 | 39.3 | 69 | 56.6 | 2 | 1.6 | 3 | 2.5 | 122 |
| | mostly | 23 | 44.2 | 23 | 44.2 | 2 | 3.8 | 4 | 7.7 | 52 |
| | never | 46 | 38.3 | 67 | 55.8 | 3 | 2.5 | 4 | 3.3 | 120 |
| | **Total** | **130** | **38.8** | **186** | **55.5** | 8 | **2.4** | 11 | **3.3** | **335** |

(Contd.)

| 1 | 2 | 3 | 4 | 5 | 6 | 7 | 8 | 9 | 10 | 11 |
|---|---|---|---|---|---|---|---|---|---|---|
| Tourist place | often | 15 | 34.9 | 26 | 60.5 | 1 | 2.3 | 1 | 2.3 | 43 |
| | some time | 41 | 35.7 | 69 | 60.0 | 3 | 2.6 | 2 | 1.7 | 115 |
| | mostly | 22 | 46.8 | 20 | 42.6 | 1 | 2.1 | 4 | 8.5 | 47 |
| | never | 47 | 37.3 | 69 | 54.8 | 5 | 4.0 | 5 | 4.0 | 126 |
| | **Total** | **125** | **37.8** | **184** | **55.6** | **10** | **3.0** | **12** | **3.6** | **331** |
| Voyage hobbies | often | 11 | 47.8 | 11 | 47.8 | 1 | 4.3 | 0 | .0 | 23 |
| | some time | 17 | 36.2 | 30 | 63.8 | 0 | .0 | 0 | .0 | 47 |
| | mostly | 12 | 40.0 | 17 | 56.7 | 1 | 3.3 | 0 | .0 | 30 |
| | never | 80 | 38.3 | 113 | 54.1 | 6 | 2.9 | 10 | 4.8 | 209 |
| | **Total** | **120** | **38.8** | **171** | **55.3** | **8** | **2.6** | **10** | **3.2** | **309** |
| Restaurant | often | 9 | 29.0 | 21 | 67.7 | 1 | 3.2 | 0 | .0 | 31 |
| | some time | 43 | 39.1 | 62 | 56.4 | 2 | 1.8 | 3 | 2.7 | 110 |
| | mostly | 27 | 42.9 | 28 | 44.4 | 3 | 4.8 | 5 | 7.9 | 63 |
| | never | 46 | 36.5 | 72 | 57.1 | 4 | 3.2 | 4 | 3.2 | 126 |
| | **Total** | **125** | **37.9** | **183** | **55.5** | **10** | **3.0** | **12** | **3.6** | **330** |
| Fast food restaurant | often | 17 | 34.0 | 32 | 64.0 | 1 | 2.0 | 0 | .0 | 50 |
| | some time | 61 | 42.7 | 77 | 53.8 | 3 | 2.1 | 2 | 1.4 | 143 |
| | mostly | 32 | 48.5 | 26 | 39.4 | 3 | 4.5 | 5 | 7.6 | 66 |

(Contd.)

| 1 | 2 | 3 | 4 | 5 | 6 | 7 | 8 | 9 | 10 | 11 |
|---|---|---|---|---|---|---|---|---|---|---|
| | never | 21 | 25.3 | 57 | 68.7 | 2 | 2.4 | 3 | 3.6 | 83 |
| | **Total** | **131** | **38.3** | **192** | **56.1** | **9** | **2.6** | **10** | **2.9** | **342** |
| Coffee shops | often | 15 | 40.5 | 20 | 54.1 | 2 | 5.4 | 0 | .0 | 37 |
| | some time | 49 | 43.8 | 60 | 53.6 | 3 | 2.7 | 0 | .0 | 112 |
| | mostly | 30 | 50.0 | 23 | 38.3 | 2 | 3.3 | 5 | 8.3 | 60 |
| | never | 32 | 27.8 | 75 | 65.2 | 3 | 2.6 | 5 | 4.3 | 115 |
| | **Total** | **126** | **38.9** | **178** | **54.9** | **10** | **3.1** | **10** | **3.1** | **324** |
| Social work | often | 20 | 40.8 | 27 | 55.1 | 2 | 4.1 | 0 | .0 | 49 |
| | some time | 50 | 41.3 | 65 | 53.7 | 4 | 3.3 | 2 | 1.7 | 121 |
| | mostly | 35 | 46.7 | 35 | 46.7 | 1 | 1.3 | 4 | 5.3 | 75 |
| | never | 23 | 25.8 | 57 | 64.0 | 3 | 3.4 | 6 | 6.7 | 89 |
| | **Total** | **128** | **38.3** | **184** | **55.1** | **10** | **3.0** | **12** | **3.6** | **334** |
| Any other | often | 13 | 41.9 | 18 | 58.1 | 0 | .0 | 0 | .0 | 31 |
| | some time | 27 | 42.9 | 35 | 55.6 | 1 | 1.6 | 0 | .0 | 63 |
| | mostly | 11 | 39.3 | 15 | 53.6 | 1 | 3.6 | 1 | 3.6 | 28 |
| | never | 12 | 23.5 | 33 | 64.7 | 3 | 5.9 | 3 | 5.9 | 51 |
| | **Total** | **63** | **36.4** | **101** | **58.4** | **5** | **2.9** | **4** | **2.3** | **173** |

(Contd.)

Table 3.5: Education and Leisure Time Activity

| *Activity* | | *Illiterate* | | *Primary* | | *Secondary* | | *Diploma* | | *Graduation and above* | | *Total* |
|---|---|---|---|---|---|---|---|---|---|---|---|---|
| | | *Freq.* | % | *Freq.* | % | *Freq.* | % | *Freq.* | % | *Freq.* | % | |
| 1 | 2 | 3 | 4 | 5 | 6 | 7 | 8 | 9 | 10 | 11 | 12 | 13 |
| Gym | often | 2 | 1.6 | 37 | 30.3 | 7 | 5.7 | 11 | 9.0 | 65 | 53.3 | 122 |
| | some time | 1 | .9 | 1 | .9 | 7 | 6.5 | 33 | 30.8 | 65 | 60.7 | 107 |
| | mostly | 0 | .0 | 0 | .0 | 0 | .0 | 2 | 22.2 | 7 | 77.8 | 9 |
| | never | 9 | 6.6 | 7 | 5.1 | 14 | 10.3 | 48 | 35.3 | 58 | 42.6 | 136 |
| | **Total** | **12** | **3.2** | **45** | **12.0** | **28** | **7.5** | **94** | **25.1** | **195** | **52.1** | **374** |
| Body building clubs | often | 0 | .0 | 5 | 12.8 | 2 | 5.1 | 10 | 25.6 | 22 | 56.4 | 39 |
| | some time | 0 | .0 | 12 | 12.6 | 0 | .0 | 26 | 27.4 | 57 | 60.0 | 95 |
| | mostly | 0 | .0 | 5 | 50.0 | 0 | .0 | 0 | .0 | 5 | 50.0 | 10 |
| | never | 12 | 6.2 | 22 | 11.3 | 23 | 11.8 | 51 | 26.2 | 87 | 44.6 | 195 |
| | **Total** | **12** | **3.5** | **44** | **13.0** | **25** | **7.4** | **87** | **25.7** | **171** | **50.4** | **339** |
| Cinema | often | 0 | .0 | 6 | 18.8 | 0 | .0 | 12 | 37.5 | 14 | 43.8 | 32 |
| | some time | 0 | .0 | 9 | 5.8 | 7 | 4.5 | 39 | 25.0 | 101 | 64.7 | 156 |
| | mostly | 0 | .0 | 3 | 25.0 | 2 | 16.7 | 4 | 33.3 | 3 | 25.0 | 12 |
| | never | 12 | 8.1 | 26 | 17.6 | 17 | 11.5 | 37 | 25.0 | 56 | 37.8 | 148 |
| | **Total** | **12** | **3.4** | **44** | **12.6** | **26** | **7.5** | **92** | **26.4** | **174** | **50.0** | **348** |

(Contd.)

| 1 | 2 | 3 | 4 | 5 | 6 | 7 | 8 | 9 | 10 | 11 | 12 | 13 |
|---|---|---|---|---|---|---|---|---|---|---|---|---|
| Public library | often | 0 | .0 | 6 | 12.5 | 1 | 2.1 | 10 | 20.8 | 31 | 64.6 | 48 |
| | some time | 0 | .0 | 18 | 11.7 | 5 | 3.2 | 34 | 22.1 | 97 | 63.0 | 154 |
| | often | 0 | .0 | 1 | 5.9 | 2 | 11.8 | 6 | 35.3 | 8 | 47.1 | 17 |
| | never | 12 | 9.4 | 16 | 12.5 | 17 | 13.3 | 40 | 31.3 | 43 | 33.6 | 128 |
| | Total | 12 | 3.5 | 41 | 11.8 | 25 | 7.2 | 90 | 25.9 | 179 | 51.6 | 347 |
| Festival | often | 0 | .0 | 6 | 18.2 | 1 | 3.0 | 8 | 24.2 | 18 | 54.5 | 33 |
| | some time | 0 | .0 | 13 | 12.6 | 3 | 2.9 | 19 | 18.4 | 68 | 66.0 | 103 |
| | mostly | 0 | .0 | 2 | 16.7 | 2 | 16.7 | 1 | 8.3 | 7 | 58.3 | 12 |
| | never | 12 | 6.6 | 21 | 11.5 | 19 | 10.4 | 57 | 31.3 | 73 | 40.1 | 182 |
| | Total | 12 | 3.6 | 42 | 12.7 | 25 | 7.6 | 85 | 25.8 | 166 | 50.3 | 330 |
| Museum | often | 0 | .0 | 6 | 23.1 | 0 | .0 | 2 | 7.7 | 18 | 69.2 | 26 |
| | sometime | 0 | .0 | 9 | 8.5 | 3 | 2.8 | 23 | 21.7 | 71 | 67.0 | 106 |
| | mostly | 0 | .0 | 1 | 10.0 | 1 | 10.0 | 1 | 10.0 | 7 | 70.0 | 10 |
| | never | 12 | 6.2 | 23 | 11.9 | 20 | 10.4 | 62 | 32.1 | 76 | 39.4 | 193 |
| | Total | 12 | 3.6 | 39 | 11.6 | 24 | 7.2 | 88 | 26.3 | 172 | 51.3 | 335 |
| Concert hall | often | 0 | .0 | 3 | 13.6 | 0 | .0 | 4 | 18.2 | 15 | 68.2 | 22 |
| | some time | 0 | .0 | 13 | 17.6 | 3 | 4.1 | 14 | 18.9 | 44 | 59.5 | 74 |
| | mostly | 0 | .0 | 2 | 8.0 | 1 | 4.0 | 4 | 16.0 | 18 | 72.0 | 25 |

(Contd.)

| 1 | 2 | 3 | 4 | 5 | 6 | 7 | 8 | 9 | 10 | 11 | 12 | 13 |
|---|---|---|---|---|---|---|---|---|---|---|---|---|
| | never | 12 | 6.2 | 23 | 11.9 | 21 | 10.8 | 58 | 29.9 | 80 | 41.2 | 194 |
| | Total | **12** | **3.8** | **41** | **13.0** | **25** | **7.9** | **80** | **25.4** | **157** | **49.8** | **315** |
| Exhibition | often | 0 | .0 | 4 | 11.8 | 2 | 5.9 | 4 | 11.8 | 24 | 70.6 | 34 |
| | sometime | 1 | .8 | 13 | 9.9 | 5 | 3.8 | 32 | 24.4 | 80 | 61.1 | 131 |
| | mostly | 0 | .0 | 0 | .0 | 1 | 1.9 | 21 | 40.4 | 30 | 57.7 | 52 |
| | never | 12 | 11.4 | 18 | 17.1 | 12 | 11.4 | 28 | 26.7 | 35 | 33.3 | 105 |
| | Total | **13** | **4.0** | **35** | **10.9** | **20** | **6.2** | **85** | **26.4** | **169** | **52.5** | **322** |
| Park | often | 0 | .0 | 7 | 11.9 | 2 | 3.4 | 14 | 23.7 | 36 | 61.0 | 59 |
| | some time | 0 | .0 | 16 | 10.3 | 6 | 3.8 | 38 | 24.4 | 96 | 61.5 | 156 |
| | mostly | 1 | 1.2 | 5 | 6.1 | 5 | 6.1 | 28 | 34.1 | 43 | 52.4 | 82 |
| | never | 12 | 20.0 | 9 | 15.0 | 11 | 18.3 | 13 | 21.7 | 15 | 25.0 | 60 |
| | Total | **13** | **3.6** | **37** | **10.4** | **24** | **6.7** | **93** | **26.1** | **190** | **53.2** | **357** |
| Historical places | often | 1 | 2.4 | 6 | 14.6 | 1 | 2.4 | 5 | 12.2 | 28 | 68.3 | 41 |
| | sometime | 0 | .0 | 14 | 12.4 | 5 | 4.4 | 17 | 15.0 | 77 | 68.1 | 113 |
| | mostly | 0 | .0 | 7 | 13.5 | 2 | 3.8 | 13 | 25.0 | 30 | 57.7 | 52 |
| | never | 11 | 9.3 | 12 | 10.2 | 15 | 12.7 | 44 | 37.3 | 36 | 30.5 | 118 |
| | Total | **12** | **3.7** | **39** | **12.0** | **23** | **7.1** | **79** | **24.4** | **171** | **52.8** | **324** |

(Contd.)

| 1 | 2 | 3 | 4 | 5 | 6 | 7 | 8 | 9 | 10 | 11 | 12 | 13 |
|---|---|---|---|---|---|---|---|---|---|---|---|---|
| Tourist place | often | 0 | .0 | 6 | 15.4 | 3 | 7.7 | 7 | 17.9 | 23 | 59.0 | 39 |
| | some time | 0 | .0 | 15 | 13.2 | 5 | 4.4 | 19 | 16.7 | 75 | 65.8 | 114 |
| | mostly | 1 | 2.1 | 2 | 4.3 | 1 | 2.1 | 15 | 31.9 | 28 | 59.6 | 47 |
| | never | 12 | 9.8 | 13 | 10.7 | 14 | 11.5 | 41 | 33.6 | 42 | 34.4 | 122 |
| | Total | 13 | 4.0 | 36 | 11.2 | 23 | 7.1 | 82 | 25.5 | 168 | 52.2 | 322 |
| Voyage hobbies | often | 0 | .0 | 7 | 36.8 | 0 | .0 | 2 | 10.5 | 10 | 52.6 | 19 |
| | some time | 0 | .0 | 10 | 25.0 | 1 | 2.5 | 3 | 7.5 | 26 | 65.0 | 40 |
| | mostly | 1 | 3.3 | 6 | 20.0 | 1 | 3.3 | 5 | 16.7 | 17 | 56.7 | 30 |
| | never | 12 | 5.7 | 14 | 6.7 | 19 | 9.0 | 68 | 32.4 | 97 | 46.2 | 210 |
| | **Total** | **13** | **4.3** | **37** | **12.4** | **21** | **7.0** | **78** | **26.1** | **150** | **50.2** | **299** |
| Restaurant | often | 0 | .0 | 2 | 6.1 | 4 | 12.1 | 7 | 21.2 | 20 | 60.6 | 33 |
| | some time | 0 | .0 | 1 | .9 | 5 | 4.5 | 38 | 34.5 | 66 | 60.0 | 110 |
| | mostly | 0 | .0 | 5 | 7.9 | 2 | 3.2 | 24 | 38.1 | 32 | 50.8 | 63 |
| | never | 12 | 10.4 | 26 | 22.6 | 12 | 10.4 | 20 | 17.4 | 45 | 39.1 | 115 |
| | **Total** | **12** | **3.7** | **34** | **10.6** | **23** | **7.2** | **89** | **27.7** | **163** | **50.8** | **321** |
| Fast food restaurant | often | 0 | .0 | 7 | 14.9 | 1 | 2.1 | 6 | 12.8 | 33 | 70.2 | 47 |
| | some time | 0 | .0 | 20 | 14.8 | 7 | 5.2 | 33 | 24.4 | 75 | 55.6 | 135 |
| | mostly | 1 | 1.5 | 2 | 3.0 | 4 | 6.0 | 23 | 34.3 | 37 | 55.2 | 67 |

(Contd.)

| 1 | 2 | 3 | 4 | 5 | 6 | 7 | 8 | 9 | 10 | 11 | 12 | 13 |
|---|---|---|---|---|---|---|---|---|---|---|---|---|
| | never | 12 | 14.5 | 9 | 10.8 | 12 | 14.5 | 24 | 28.9 | 26 | 31.3 | 83 |
| | **Total** | **13** | **3.9** | **38** | **11.4** | **24** | **7.2** | **86** | **25.9** | **171** | **51.5** | **332** |
| Coffee shops | often | 0 | .0 | 7 | 19.4 | 0 | .0 | 7 | 19.4 | 22 | 61.1 | 36 |
| | some time | 0 | .0 | 14 | 12.8 | 6 | 5.5 | 22 | 20.2 | 67 | 61.5 | 109 |
| | mostly | 0 | .0 | 5 | 8.5 | 4 | 6.8 | 22 | 37.3 | 28 | 47.5 | 59 |
| | never | 12 | 10.7 | 13 | 11.6 | 14 | 12.5 | 30 | 26.8 | 43 | 38.4 | 112 |
| | **Total** | **12** | **3.8** | **39** | **12.3** | **24** | **7.6** | **81** | **25.6** | **160** | **50.6** | **316** |
| Social work | often | 0 | .0 | 3 | 6.0 | 3 | 6.0 | 14 | 28.0 | 30 | 60.0 | 50 |
| | some time | 0 | .0 | 13 | 11.4 | 6 | 5.3 | 22 | 19.3 | 73 | 64.0 | 114 |
| | mostly | 1 | 1.3 | 9 | 11.8 | 3 | 3.9 | 22 | 28.9 | 41 | 53.9 | 76 |
| | never | 12 | 13.8 | 12 | 13.8 | 9 | 10.3 | 25 | 28.7 | 29 | 33.3 | 87 |
| | **Total** | **13** | **4.0** | **37** | **11.3** | **21** | **6.4** | **83** | **25.4** | **173** | **52.9** | **327** |
| Any other | often | 0 | .0 | 6 | 18.8 | 3 | 9.4 | 7 | 21.9 | 16 | 50.0 | 32 |
| | some time | 0 | .0 | 13 | 25.0 | 3 | 5.8 | 4 | 7.7 | 32 | 61.5 | 52 |
| | mostly | 1 | 2.9 | 5 | 14.7 | 4 | 11.8 | 8 | 23.5 | 16 | 47.1 | 34 |
| | never | 9 | 18.4 | 8 | 16.3 | 5 | 10.2 | 14 | 28.6 | 13 | 26.5 | 49 |
| | **Total** | **10** | **6.0** | **32** | **19.2** | **15** | **9.0** | **33** | **19.8** | **77** | **46.1** | **167** |

(Contd.)

Table 3.6 : Income and Leisure Time Activities

| *Activities* | | *No income* | | *Below1000* | | *1001-3000* | | *3001-6000* | | *6001 and above* | | |
|---|---|---|---|---|---|---|---|---|---|---|---|---|
| | | *Freq.* | *%* | *Freq.* | *%* | *Freq.* | *%* | *Freq.* | *%* | *Freq.* | *%* | *Total* |
| 1 | 2 | 3 | 4 | 5 | 6 | 7 | 8 | 9 | 10 | 11 | 12 | 13 |
| Gym | often | 34 | 24.3 | 18 | 12.9 | 17 | 12.1 | 13 | 9.3 | 58 | 41.4 | 140 |
| | some time | 34 | 33.7 | 2 | 2.0 | 32 | 31.7 | 19 | 18.8 | 14 | 13.9 | 101 |
| | mostly | 5 | 55.6 | 0 | .0 | 2 | 22.2 | 2 | 22.2 | 0 | .0 | 9 |
| | never | 59 | 44.7 | 20 | 15.2 | 36 | 27.3 | 9 | 6.8 | 8 | 6.1 | 132 |
| | Total | **132** | **34.6** | **40** | **10.5** | **87** | **22.8** | **43** | **11.3** | **80** | **20.9** | **382** |
| Body building clubs | often | 10 | 23.8 | 3 | 7.1 | 10 | 23.8 | 6 | 14.3 | 13 | 31.0 | 42 |
| | some time | 26 | 26.3 | 7 | 7.1 | 21 | 21.2 | 12 | 12.1 | 33 | 33.3 | 99 |
| | mostly | 4 | 40.0 | 0 | .0 | 1 | 10.0 | 2 | 20.0 | 3 | 30.0 | 10 |
| | never | 88 | 44.2 | 28 | 14.1 | 42 | 21.1 | 18 | 9.0 | 23 | 11.6 | 199 |
| | Total | **128** | **36.6** | **38** | **10.9** | **74** | **21.1** | **38** | **10.9** | **72** | **20.6** | **350** |
| Cinema- | often | 15 | 45.5 | 1 | 3.0 | 7 | 21.2 | 1 | 3.0 | 9 | 27.3 | 33 |
| | some time | 55 | 35.7 | 14 | 9.1 | 33 | 21.4 | 23 | 14.9 | 29 | 18.8 | 154 |
| | mostly | 8 | 66.7 | 2 | 16.7 | 0 | .0 | 2 | 16.7 | 0 | .0 | 12 |
| | never | 57 | 36.3 | 21 | 13.4 | 32 | 20.4 | 15 | 9.6 | 32 | 20.4 | 157 |
| | Total | **135** | **37.9** | **38** | **10.7** | **72** | **20.2** | **41** | **11.5** | **70** | **19.7** | **356** |

(Contd.)

| 1 | 2 | 3 | 4 | 5 | 6 | 7 | 8 | 9 | 10 | 11 | 12 | 13 |
|---|---|---|---|---|---|---|---|---|---|---|---|---|
| Public library | often | 18 | 36.0 | 6 | 12.0 | 8 | 16.0 | 4 | 8.0 | 14 | 28.0 | 50 |
| | some time | 52 | 33.1 | 14 | 8.9 | 29 | 18.5 | 19 | 12.1 | 43 | 27.4 | 157 |
| | often | 8 | 42.1 | 2 | 10.5 | 1 | 5.3 | 4 | 21.1 | 4 | 21.1 | 19 |
| | never | 54 | 41.5 | 20 | 15.4 | 33 | 25.4 | 10 | 7.7 | 13 | 10.0 | 130 |
| | **Total** | **132** | **37.1** | **42** | **11.8** | **71** | **19.9** | **37** | **10.4** | **74** | **20.8** | **356** |
| Festival | often | 14 | 36.8 | 2 | 5.3 | 7 | 18.4 | 2 | 5.3 | 13 | 34.2 | 38 |
| | some time | 31 | 29.0 | 11 | 10.3 | 13 | 12.1 | 20 | 18.7 | 32 | 29.9 | 107 |
| | mostly | 2 | 15.4 | 2 | 15.4 | 0 | .0 | 4 | 30.8 | 5 | 38.5 | 13 |
| | never | 80 | 43.7 | 23 | 12.6 | 46 | 25.1 | 14 | 7.7 | 20 | 10.9 | 183 |
| | **Total** | **127** | **37.2** | **38** | **11.1** | **66** | **19.4** | **40** | **11.7** | **70** | **20.5** | **341** |
| Museum | often | 10 | 35.7 | 0 | .0 | 6 | 21.4 | 0 | .0 | 12 | 42.9 | 28 |
| | sometime | 28 | 27.2 | 8 | 7.8 | 18 | 17.5 | 21 | 20.4 | 28 | 27.2 | 103 |
| | mostly | 3 | 27.3 | 1 | 9.1 | 0 | .0 | 2 | 18.2 | 5 | 45.5 | 11 |
| | never | 89 | 44.3 | 29 | 14.4 | 43 | 21.4 | 15 | 7.5 | 25 | 12.4 | 201 |
| | **Total** | 130 | **37.9** | **38** | **11.1** | **67** | **19.5** | **38** | 11.1 | **70** | **20.4** | **343** |
| Concerthall | often | 10 | 50.0 | 1 | 5.0 | 1 | 5.0 | 3 | 15.0 | 5 | 25.0 | 20 |
| | some time | 23 | 29.1 | 7 | 8.9 | 11 | 13.9 | 13 | 16.5 | 25 | 31.6 | 79 |
| | mostly | 4 | 16.0 | 3 | 12.0 | 2 | 8.0 | 5 | 20.0 | 11 | 44.0 | 25 |

(Contd.)

| 1 | 2 | 3 | 4 | 5 | 6 | 7 | 8 | 9 | 10 | 11 | 12 | 13 |
|---|---|---|---|---|---|---|---|---|---|---|---|---|
| | never | 88 | 44.2 | 25 | 12.6 | 45 | 22.6 | 12 | 6.0 | 29 | 14.6 | 199 |
| | **Total** | **125** | **38.7** | **36** | **11.1** | **59** | **18.3** | **33** | **10.2** | **70** | **21.7** | **323** |
| Exhibition | often | 13 | 40.6 | 2 | 6.3 | 5 | 15.6 | 5 | 15.6 | 7 | 21.9 | 32 |
| | sometime | 47 | 35.6 | 13 | 9.8 | 39 | 29.5 | 14 | 10.6 | 19 | 14.4 | 132 |
| | mostly | 15 | 30.0 | 4 | 8.0 | 6 | 12.0 | 10 | 20.0 | 15 | 30.0 | 50 |
| | never | 54 | 47.0 | 17 | 14.8 | 18 | 15.7 | 8 | 7.0 | 18 | 15.7 | 115 |
| | **Total** | **129** | **39.2** | **36** | **10.9** | **68** | **20.7** | **37** | **11.2** | **59** | **17.9** | **329** |
| Park | often | 25 | 41.7 | 5 | 8.3 | 13 | 21.7 | 5 | 8.3 | 12 | 20.0 | 60 |
| | some time | 49 | 31.6 | 15 | 9.7 | 40 | 25.8 | 22 | 14.2 | 29 | 18.7 | 155 |
| | mostly | 27 | 32.9 | 7 | 8.5 | 17 | 20.7 | 10 | 12.2 | 21 | 25.6 | 82 |
| | never | 35 | 53.0 | 12 | 18.2 | 11 | 16.7 | 3 | 4.5 | 5 | 7.6 | 66 |
| | **Total** | **136** | **37.5** | **39** | **10.7** | **81** | **22.3** | **40** | **11.0** | **67** | **18.5** | **363** |
| Historical places | often | 12 | 30.0 | 4 | 10.0 | 7 | 17.5 | 3 | 7.5 | 14 | 35.0 | 40 |
| | sometime | 37 | 31.1 | 8 | 6.7 | 28 | 23.5 | 18 | 15.1 | 28 | 23.5 | 119 |
| | mostly | 12 | 22.6 | 4 | 7.5 | 3 | 5.7 | 13 | 24.5 | 21 | 39.6 | 53 |
| | never | 66 | 54.5 | 20 | 16.5 | 24 | 19.8 | 6 | 5.0 | 5 | 4.1 | 121 |
| | **Total** | **127** | **38.1** | **36** | **10.8** | **62** | **18.6** | **40** | **12.0** | **68** | **20.4** | **333** |

(Contd.)

| 1 | 2 | 3 | 4 | 5 | 6 | 7 | 8 | 9 | 10 | 11 | 12 | 13 |
|---|---|---|---|---|---|---|---|---|---|---|---|---|
| Touristyplace | often | 18 | 42.9 | 4 | 9.5 | 4 | 9.5 | 6 | 14.3 | 10 | 23.8 | 42 |
| | some time | 39 | 34.8 | 8 | 7.1 | 31 | 27.7 | 13 | 11.6 | 21 | 18.8 | 112 |
| | mostly | 17 | 34.0 | 4 | 8.0 | 4 | 8.0 | 10 | 20.0 | 15 | 30.0 | 50 |
| | never | 57 | 44.5 | 21 | 16.4 | 24 | 18.8 | 8 | 6.3 | 18 | 14.1 | 128 |
| | **Total** | **131** | **39.5** | **37** | **11.1** | **63** | **19.0** | **37** | **11.1** | **64** | **19.3** | **332** |
| Voyage hobbies | often | 5 | 21.7 | 4 | 17.4 | 2 | 8.7 | 2 | 8.7 | 10 | 43.5 | 23 |
| | some time | 14 | 31.1 | 2 | 4.4 | 7 | 15.6 | 4 | 8.9 | 18 | 40.0 | 45 |
| | mostly | 10 | 34.5 | 2 | 6.9 | 1 | 3.4 | 4 | 13.8 | 12 | 41.4 | 29 |
| | never | 95 | 45.0 | 27 | 12.8 | 46 | 21.8 | 22 | 10.4 | 21 | 10.0 | 211 |
| | **Total** | **124** | **40.3** | **35** | **11.4** | **56** | **18.2** | **32** | **10.4** | **61** | **19.8** | **308** |
| Restaurant | often | 15 | 48.4 | 3 | 9.7 | 8 | 25.8 | 2 | 6.5 | 3 | 9.7 | 31 |
| | some time | 45 | 40.5 | 11 | 9.9 | 29 | 26.1 | 14 | 12.6 | 12 | 10.8 | 111 |
| | mostly | 19 | 31.1 | 7 | 11.5 | 8 | 13.1 | 10 | 16.4 | 17 | 27.9 | 61 |
| | never | 50 | 39.7 | 15 | 11.9 | 21 | 16.7 | 11 | 8.7 | 29 | 23.0 | 126 |
| | **Total** | **129** | **39.2** | **36** | **10.9** | **66** | **20.1** | **37** | **11.2** | **61** | **18.5** | **329** |
| Fast food restaurant | often | 16 | 33.3 | 2 | 4.2 | 8 | 16.7 | 7 | 14.6 | 15 | 31.3 | 48 |
| | some time | 52 | 36.6 | 19 | 13.4 | 30 | 21.1 | 16 | 11.3 | 25 | 17.6 | 142 |
| | mostly | 19 | 29.2 | 7 | 10.8 | 8 | 12.3 | 10 | 15.4 | 21 | 32.3 | 65 |

(Contd.)

| 1 | 2 | 3 | 4 | 5 | 6 | 7 | 8 | 9 | 10 | 11 | 12 | 13 |
|---|---|---|---|---|---|---|---|---|---|---|---|---|
| | never | 42 | 48.3 | 14 | 16.1 | 19 | 21.8 | 7 | 8.0 | 5 | 5.7 | 87 |
| | **Total** | **129** | **37.7** | **42** | **12.3** | **65** | **19.0** | **40** | **11.7** | **66** | **19.3** | **342** |
| Coffee-shops | often | 12 | 33.3 | 3 | 8.3 | 3 | 8.3 | 2 | 5.6 | 16 | 44.4 | 36 |
| | some time | 44 | 37.9 | 9 | 7.8 | 31 | 26.7 | 12 | 10.3 | 20 | 17.2 | 116 |
| | mostly | 17 | 29.8 | 7 | 12.3 | 6 | 10.5 | 9 | 15.8 | 18 | 31.6 | 57 |
| | never | 57 | 49.1 | 18 | 15.5 | 22 | 19.0 | 11 | 9.5 | 8 | 6.9 | 116 |
| | **Total** | **130** | **40.0** | **37** | **11.4** | **62** | **19.1** | **34** | **10.5** | **62** | **19.1** | **325** |
| Social work | often | 17 | 34.7 | 7 | 14.3 | 13 | 26.5 | 2 | 4.1 | 10 | 20.4 | 49 |
| | some time | 42 | 34.4 | 10 | 8.2 | 25 | 20.5 | 18 | 14.8 | 27 | 22.1 | 122 |
| | mostly | 25 | 33.3 | 5 | 6.7 | 15 | 20.0 | 10 | 13.3 | 20 | 26.7 | 75 |
| | never | 41 | 46.1 | 15 | 16.9 | 16 | 18.0 | 8 | 9.0 | 9 | 10.1 | 89 |
| | **Total** | **125** | **37.3** | **37** | **11.0** | **69** | **20.6** | **38** | **11.3** | **66** | **19.7** | **335** |
| Any other | often | 7 | 21.9 | 4 | 12.5 | 12 | 37.5 | 4 | 12.5 | 5 | 15.6 | 32 |
| | some time | 21 | 32.8 | 6 | 9.4 | 13 | 20.3 | 7 | 10.9 | 17 | 26.6 | 64 |
| | mostly | 10 | 30.3 | 3 | 9.1 | 7 | 21.2 | 1 | 3.0 | 12 | 36.4 | 33 |
| | never | 23 | 44.2 | 10 | 19.2 | 10 | 19.2 | 4 | 7.7 | 5 | 9.6 | 52 |
| | **Total** | **61** | **33.7** | **23** | **12.7** | **42** | **23.2** | **16** | **8.8** | **39** | **21.5** | **181** |

(Contd.)

Table 3.7 : Occupation and Leisure Time Activities

| Activities | | *Unemployed* | | *Self employed clerk, business women* | | *Students* | | *Teacher, principal, govt. officer* | | *Doctor, engineer, lawyer, professor* | | *Total* |
|---|---|---|---|---|---|---|---|---|---|---|---|---|
| 1 | 2 | 3 | | 4 | | 5 | | 6 | | 7 | | 8 |
| Gym | often | 19 | 13.9 | 38 | 27.7 | 5 | 3.6 | 21 | 15.3 | 54 | 39.4 | 137 |
| | some time | 16 | 15.1 | 20 | 18.9 | 15 | 14.2 | 37 | 34.9 | 18 | 17.0 | 106 |
| | mostly | 2 | 22.2 | 0 | .0 | 3 | 33.3 | 4 | 44.4 | 0 | .0 | 9 |
| | never | 43 | 31.4 | 32 | 23.4 | 17 | 12.4 | 39 | 28.5 | 6 | 4.4 | 137 |
| | **Total** | **80** | **20.6** | **90** | **23.1** | **40** | **10.3** | **101** | **26.0** | **78** | **20.1** | **389** |
| Body building clubs | often | 7 | 17.1 | 8 | 19.5 | 3 | 7.3 | 12 | 29.3 | 11 | 26.8 | 41 |
| | some time | 17 | 16.5 | 20 | 19.4 | 6 | 5.8 | 23 | 22.3 | 37 | 35.9 | 103 |
| | mostly | 1 | 10.0 | 5 | 50.0 | 1 | 10.0 | 1 | 10.0 | 2 | 20.0 | 10 |
| | never | 53 | 26.5 | 50 | 25.0 | 28 | 14.0 | 49 | 24.5 | 20 | 10.0 | 200 |
| | **Total** | **78** | **22.0** | **83** | **23.4** | **38** | **10.7** | **85** | **24.0** | **70** | **19.8** | **354** |
| Cinema | often | 9 | 28.1 | 8 | 25.0 | 6 | 18.8 | 3 | 9.4 | 6 | 18.8 | 32 |
| | some time | 25 | 15.4 | 28 | 17.3 | 27 | 16.7 | 54 | 33.3 | 28 | 17.3 | 162 |
| | mostly | 2 | 18.2 | 4 | 36.4 | 4 | 36.4 | 1 | 9.1 | 0 | .0 | 11 |
| | never | 45 | 28.8 | 44 | 28.2 | 5 | 3.2 | 30 | 19.2 | 32 | 20.5 | 156 |
| | **Total** | **81** | **22.4** | **84** | **23.3** | **42** | **11.6** | **88** | **24.4** | **66** | **18.3** | **361** |

(Contd.)

| 1 | 2 | 3 | | 4 | | 5 | | 6 | | 7 | | 8 |
|---|---|---|---|---|---|---|---|---|---|---|---|---|
| Public library | often | 9 | 17.3 | 11 | 21.2 | 10 | 19.2 | 12 | 23.1 | 10 | 19.2 | 52 |
| | some time | 22 | 13.7 | 30 | 18.6 | 24 | 14.9 | 37 | 23.0 | 48 | 29.8 | 161 |
| | often | 2 | 11.1 | 5 | 27.8 | 2 | 11.1 | 8 | 44.4 | 1 | 5.6 | 18 |
| | never | 47 | 35.6 | 34 | 25.8 | 6 | 4.5 | 29 | 22.0 | 16 | 12.1 | 132 |
| | **Total** | **80** | **22.0** | **80** | **22.0** | **42** | **11.6** | **86** | **23.7** | **75** | **20.7** | **363** |
| Festival | often | 3 | 8.3 | 8 | 22.2 | 8 | 22.2 | 5 | 13.9 | 12 | 33.3 | 36 |
| | some time | 14 | 12.8 | 22 | 20.2 | 9 | 8.3 | 27 | 24.8 | 37 | 33.9 | 109 |
| | mostly | 1 | 9.1 | 2 | 18.2 | 0 | .0 | 7 | 63.6 | 1 | 9.1 | 11 |
| | never | 60 | 32.1 | 47 | 25.1 | 20 | 10.7 | 41 | 21.9 | 19 | 10.2 | 187 |
| | **Total** | **78** | **22.7** | **79** | **23.0** | **37** | **10.8** | **80** | **23.3** | **69** | **20.1** | **343** |
| Museum | often | 1 | 3.8 | 4 | 15.4 | 7 | 26.9 | 7 | 26.9 | 7 | 26.9 | 26 |
| | sometime | 19 | 17.8 | 16 | 15.0 | 10 | 9.3 | 35 | 32.7 | 27 | 25.2 | 107 |
| | mostly | 1 | 9.1 | 2 | 18.2 | 1 | 9.1 | 7 | 63.6 | 0 | .0 | 11 |
| | never | 58 | 28.4 | 53 | 26.0 | 22 | 10.8 | 37 | 18.1 | 34 | 16.7 | 204 |
| | **Total** | **79** | **22.7** | **75** | **21.6** | **40** | **11.5** | **86** | **24.7** | **68** | **19.5** | **348** |
| Concert hall | often | 5 | 22.7 | 3 | 13.6 | 6 | 27.3 | 4 | 18.2 | 4 | 18.2 | 22 |
| | some time | 10 | 12.7 | 21 | 26.6 | 7 | 8.9 | 18 | 22.8 | 23 | 29.1 | 79 |
| | mostly | 5 | 19.2 | 3 | 11.5 | 0 | .0 | 9 | 34.6 | 9 | 34.6 | 26 |

(Contd.)

| 1 | 2 | 3 | | 4 | | 5 | | 6 | | 7 | | 8 |
|---|---|---|---|---|---|---|---|---|---|---|---|---|
| | never | 58 | 28.9 | 49 | 24.4 | 24 | 11.9 | 40 | 19.9 | 30 | 14.9 | 201 |
| | **Total** | **78** | **23.8** | **76** | **23.2** | **37** | **11.3** | **71** | **21.6** | **66** | **20.1** | **328** |
| Exhibition | often | 4 | 12.1 | 5 | 15.2 | 8 | 24.2 | 10 | 30.3 | 6 | 18.2 | 33 |
| | sometime | 23 | 17.3 | 26 | 19.5 | 20 | 15.0 | 44 | 33.1 | 20 | 15.0 | 133 |
| | mostly | 9 | 16.4 | 8 | 14.5 | 9 | 16.4 | 18 | 32.7 | 11 | 20.0 | 55 |
| | never | 42 | 36.8 | 32 | 28.1 | 4 | 3.5 | 14 | 12.3 | 22 | 19.3 | 114 |
| | **Total** | **78** | **23.3** | **71** | **21.2** | **41** | **12.2** | **86** | **25.7** | **59** | **17.6** | **335** |
| Park | often | 13 | 21.7 | 12 | 20.0 | 10 | 16.7 | 14 | 23.3 | 11 | 18.3 | 60 |
| | some time | 25 | 16.0 | 32 | 20.5 | 17 | 10.9 | 51 | 32.7 | 31 | 19.9 | 156 |
| | mostly | 15 | 17.2 | 15 | 17.2 | 12 | 13.8 | 23 | 26.4 | 22 | 25.3 | 87 |
| | never | 30 | 46.9 | 18 | 28.1 | 2 | 3.1 | 10 | 15.6 | 4 | 6.3 | 64 |
| | **Total** | **83** | **22.6** | **77** | **21.0** | **41** | **11.2** | **98** | **26.7** | **68** | **18.5** | **367** |
| Historical places | often | 5 | 11.4 | 11 | 25.0 | 5 | 11.4 | 13 | 29.5 | 10 | 22.7 | 44 |
| | sometime | 17 | 14.3 | 15 | 12.6 | 17 | 14.3 | 35 | 29.4 | 35 | 29.4 | 119 |
| | mostly | 8 | 14.8 | 11 | 20.4 | 3 | 5.6 | 15 | 27.8 | 17 | 31.5 | 54 |
| | never | 47 | 38.5 | 34 | 27.9 | 13 | 10.7 | 19 | 15.6 | 9 | 7.4 | 122 |
| | Total | 77 | 22.7 | 71 | 20.9 | 38 | 11.2 | 82 | 24.2 | 71 | 20.9 | 339 |

(Contd.)

| 1 | 2 | 3 | | 4 | | 5 | | 6 | | 7 | | 8 |
|---|---|---|---|---|---|---|---|---|---|---|---|---|
| Tourist place | often | 7 | 16.3 | 6 | 14.0 | 9 | 20.9 | 10 | 23.3 | 11 | 25.6 | 43 |
| | some time | 20 | 17.7 | 19 | 16.8 | 15 | 13.3 | 36 | 31.9 | 23 | 20.4 | 113 |
| | mostly | 8 | 15.7 | 9 | 17.6 | 7 | 13.7 | 13 | 25.5 | 14 | 27.5 | 51 |
| | never | 47 | 36.4 | 35 | 27.1 | 7 | 5.4 | 22 | 17.1 | 18 | 14.0 | 129 |
| | **Total** | **82** | **24.4** | **69** | **20.5** | **38** | **11.3** | **81** | **24.1** | **66** | **19.6** | **336** |
| Voyage hobbies | often | 2 | 8.7 | 7 | 30.4 | 3 | 13.0 | 5 | 21.7 | 6 | 26.1 | 23 |
| | some time | 8 | 19.0 | 5 | 11.9 | 3 | 7.1 | 6 | 14.3 | 20 | 47.6 | 42 |
| | mostly | 7 | 23.3 | 6 | 20.0 | 2 | 6.7 | 3 | 10.0 | 12 | 40.0 | 30 |
| | never | 60 | 27.6 | 49 | 22.6 | 28 | 12.9 | 57 | 26.3 | 23 | 10.6 | 217 |
| | **Total** | **77** | **24.7** | **67** | **21.5** | **36** | **11.5** | **71** | **22.8** | **61** | **19.6** | **312** |
| Restaurant | often | 8 | 24.2 | 8 | 24.2 | 7 | 21.2 | 7 | 21.2 | 3 | 9.1 | 33 |
| | some time | 19 | 17.0 | 25 | 22.3 | 20 | 17.9 | 35 | 31.3 | 13 | 11.6 | 112 |
| | mostly | 14 | 21.5 | 13 | 20.0 | 6 | 9.2 | 18 | 27.7 | 14 | 21.5 | 65 |
| | never | 37 | 29.8 | 29 | 23.4 | 8 | 6.5 | 19 | 15.3 | 31 | 25.0 | 124 |
| | **Total** | **78** | **23.4** | **75** | **22.5** | **41** | **12.3** | **79** | **23.7** | **61** | **18.3** | **334** |
| Fast food restaurant | often | 8 | 16.3 | 8 | 16.3 | 6 | 12.2 | 13 | 26.5 | 14 | 28.6 | 49 |
| | some time | 21 | 15.1 | 34 | 24.5 | 21 | 15.1 | 32 | 23.0 | 31 | 22.3 | 139 |
| | mostly | 15 | 21.4 | 11 | 15.7 | 6 | 8.6 | 21 | 30.0 | 17 | 24.3 | 70 |

(Contd.)

| 1 | 2 | 3 | | 4 | | 5 | | 6 | | 7 | | 8 |
|---|---|---|---|---|---|---|---|---|---|---|---|---|
| | never | 35 | 39.8 | 22 | 25.0 | 5 | 5.7 | 19 | 21.6 | 7 | 8.0 | 88 |
| | **Total** | **79** | **22.8** | **75** | **21.7** | **38** | **11.0** | **85** | **24.6** | **69** | **19.9** | **346** |
| Coffee shops | often | 3 | 8.1 | 10 | 27.0 | 9 | 24.3 | 5 | 13.5 | 10 | 27.0 | 37 |
| | some time | 24 | 21.2 | 17 | 15.0 | 16 | 14.2 | 26 | 23.0 | 30 | 26.5 | 113 |
| | mostly | 13 | 21.0 | 16 | 25.8 | 4 | 6.5 | 15 | 24.2 | 14 | 22.6 | 62 |
| | never | 38 | 32.8 | 31 | 26.7 | 11 | 9.5 | 25 | 21.6 | 11 | 9.5 | 116 |
| | **Total** | **78** | **23.8** | **74** | **22.6** | **40** | **12.2** | **71** | **21.6** | **65** | **19.8** | **328** |
| Social work | often | 7 | 13.5 | 13 | 25.0 | 7 | 13.5 | 14 | 26.9 | 11 | 21.2 | 52 |
| | some time | 22 | 17.9 | 21 | 17.1 | 16 | 13.0 | 33 | 26.8 | 31 | 25.2 | 123 |
| | mostly | 15 | 19.7 | 14 | 18.4 | 7 | 9.2 | 22 | 28.9 | 18 | 23.7 | 76 |
| | never | 35 | 38.5 | 25 | 27.5 | 6 | 6.6 | 15 | 16.5 | 10 | 11.0 | 91 |
| | **Total** | **79** | **23.1** | **73** | **21.3** | **36** | **10.5** | **84** | **24.6** | **70** | **20.5** | **342** |
| Any other | often | 3 | 9.4 | 9 | 28.1 | 4 | 12.5 | 11 | 34.4 | 5 | 15.6 | 32 |
| | some time | 11 | 18.0 | 12 | 19.7 | 6 | 9.8 | 14 | 23.0 | 18 | 29.5 | 61 |
| | mostly | 4 | 12.1 | 8 | 24.2 | 3 | 9.1 | 9 | 27.3 | 9 | 27.3 | 33 |
| | never | 22 | 42.3 | 17 | 32.7 | 0 | .0 | 7 | 13.5 | 6 | 11.5 | 52 |
| | **Total** | **40** | **22.5** | **46** | **25.8** | **13** | **7.3** | **41** | **23.0** | **38** | **21.3** | **178** |

(Contd.)

with their work at home.

The frequency of leisure time pattern is cross-tabulated against the level of age, marital status, education, income and occupation, of the respondents. (Table 3.3 to 3.7)

The result of cross- tabulations show that attainments of the younger ages are high. Also, we found out that in these patterns, married women participated more than unmarried women. Moreover, highly educated women participated more. Furthermore the table reveals that women with "no income" have more attendants. Finally, in "occupation" item, the table shows that "unemployed women" have attainments as well as teachers, principles and government officers. "Teacher, principle, government officer" have more attainment.

## II. RECREATION

'Recreation': Parker (1976:29), in his study, said 'recreation is a term that is often used to mean something similar to leisure. Recreation always indicates activity of some kind and, like leisure and play, it takes no single form. In its literal sense of re-creation, it may be seen as one of the functions of leisure; that of renewing the self or preparation for work. It is this element in recreation that has most commended itself to those who disapprove of 'wasted' or 'dissipated' leisure, an attitude that is positively summed up in the phrase ' wholesome recreation'. But it is also this very value-laden element in recreation that has led critics to compare it unfavonrably with leisure'. Thelma McCormack (1971) writes: Recreation is a system of social control, and like all systems of social control, it is to some degree manipulative, coercive and indoctrinating. Leisure is not.

Miller and Robinson (1963:9) believe that 'leisure and recreation and play are cultural universals, being found as common elements in the behavionr of individuals in all societies'.

R. Carlson (1972) stated: 'Recreation' is spending time in an unprofitable way. In many ways, also, a therapeutic relief of one's body or mind. And 'leisure' is most seemingly a form of entertainment or rest, while recreation is functioning for the participant but in a refreshing and pleasant manner. Today, with regard to the machinery in the modern world, the need for recreation has grown. "According to Carlson, recreation can either weaken or strengthen family ties". Parker (1976) says however, recreation can and should serve to strengthen a family and keep it together; it is possible through leisure-time pursuits to maintain family solidarity and unity of purpose.

Jain Brothers (1984) pointed out that in commercial recreation, both working and nonworking seemed to be participating almost equally, and both women in reading periodicals and newspapers, attending fewer movies while they displayed more interest in organized games. The data show in that project, mutual visits friends and neighbours were most frequent. He said, as against the non-working women, a relatively larger proportion of working women reported that they didn't get any time for recreation.

The frequency of recreation of pattern is cross-tabulated against the level of age, marital status, education, income and occupation, of the respondents in Table 3.8 to 3.10.

**Table 3.8: Recreation Pattern**

| *Recreation Pattern* | *Often* | | *Some time* | | *Mostly* | | *Never* | | *Total* |
|---|---|---|---|---|---|---|---|---|---|
| | **Freq.** | **%** | **Freq.** | **%** | **Freq.** | **%** | **Freq.** | **%** | |
| Chatting with people | 43 | 14.1 | 87 | 28.4 | 33 | 10.8 | 143 | 46.7 | 306 |
| Attending parties | 67 | 16.8 | 206 | 51.6 | 68 | 17.0 | 58 | 14.5 | 399 |
| Visiting neighbours | 60 | 15.8 | 208 | 54.7 | 53 | 13.9 | 59 | 15.5 | 380 |
| Visiting clubs | 22 | 6.4 | 85 | 24.6 | 23 | 6.7 | 215 | 62.3 | 345 |
| Visiting different organizations | 22 | 6.6 | 76 | 23.0 | 15 | 4.5 | 218 | 65.9 | 331 |
| Skin clinic | 27 | 8.0 | 97 | 28.9 | 12 | 3.6 | 200 | 59.5 | 336 |
| Any other | 24 | 13.5 | 51 | 28.7 | 7 | 3.9 | 96 | 53.9 | 178 |

The Table 3.8 reveals that the highest percentages of the women are visiting. Nearly (84.5%) of the respondents attend parties and visit neighbours. Also, around half of the women (53.3%) remarked that they chat with people. And over (34%) of respondents said that, they spend their recreation in skin clinic, attending meetings in different organizations including clubs.

**Table 3.9: Family Recreation**

| *Family Recreation Pattern* | *Often* | | *Some time* | | *Mostly* | | *Never* | | *Total* |
|---|---|---|---|---|---|---|---|---|---|
| | *Freq.* | *%* | *Freq.* | *%* | *Freq.* | *%* | *Freq.* | *%* | |
| Visiting relative | 114 | 31.2 | 152 | 41.6 | 74 | 20.3 | 25 | 6.8 | 365 |
| Organized game at home | 68 | 18.6 | 150 | 41.0 | 56 | 15.3 | 92 | 25.1 | 366 |
| Listening to radio | 60 | 16.5 | 165 | 45.3 | 28 | 7.7 | 111 | 30.5 | 364 |
| Reading newspaper or magazine | 86 | 21.8 | 195 | 49.4 | 60 | 15.2 | 54 | 13.7 | 395 |
| Recreation with children | 88 | 22.1 | 148 | 37.2 | 94 | 23.6 | 68 | 17.1 | 398 |
| Any other | 30 | 16.9 | 70 | 39.3 | 36 | 20.2 | 42 | 23.6 | 178 |

Table 3.9 shows clearly that a large number of our respondents around (93.2%) are interested in visiting relatives and organized games at home. More than (82.4%) answered "reading newspaper, magazine, and recreation with children"; almost 69.5% answered "listening to radio".

And in the other activities and rest, the larger number of women over 86.6% answered "studying". There were 71.3% of the respondents who said they attend religious activities. Moreover, 53.3% declared that they like chess, sewing, knitting, embroidery works and, 94.8% replied that they like to take rest.

To understand the recreational urban pattern of women in Iran, different parameters such as visiting, family recreation, other activities, and rest were studied.

**Table 3.10: Other Activities and Rest**

| *Other Activities* | *Often* | | *Some time* | | *Mostly* | | *Never* | | *Total* |
|---|---|---|---|---|---|---|---|---|---|
| | *Freq.* | *%* | *Freq.* | *%* | *Freq.* | *%* | *Freq.* | *%* | |
| Sewing knitting embroidery work | 44 | 14.1 | 110 | 35.1 | 30 | 9.6 | 129 | 41.2 | 313 |
| Religious activity | 52 | 14.1 | 172 | 46.6 | 39 | 10.6 | 106 | 28.7 | 369 |
| Study | 100 | 24.9 | 168 | 41.8 | 80 | 19.9 | 54 | 13.4 | 402 |
| Chess | 50 | 14.2 | 99 | 28.2 | 38 | 10.8 | 164 | 46.7 | 351 |
| Any other | 21 | 12.8 | 45 | 27.4 | 8 | 4.9 | 90 | 54.9 | 164 |
| Rest | 107 | 29.4 | 208 | 57.1 | 30 | 8.2 | 19 | 5.2 | 364 |

The results of cross-tabulations show the high attainments which is significance in the frequency of recreation pattern among respondents, with visiting (attending parties, visiting neighbours, visiting clubs) and in family recreation (organized games at home, reading newspapers, magazines, recreation with children and other activities (study, chess and rest). Also, we found out that in these patterns, married women participated more than unmarried women. Finally, in age item table shows that women have attainments as well as study, religious activities and reading newspapers, magazines have more attainment.

Statistically speaking, there is a meaningful relationship between patterns of spending recreation with age, marital status, education, income, and occupation very strongly.

Table 3.8 data of recreation pattern shows that the majority of the respondents attend in parties and visit neighbours. Also some of them spend their leisure time by chatting with people, visiting clubs and visiting different organizations and skin clinic.

In family recreation most of the respondents were interested to visit their relatives and organizing games at home. Furthermore, this research shows that women are eager to listen to the radio, read newspaper or magazine and play with children.

The research revealed that most of the respondents preferred to take rest. And, they also participate in other activities such as sewing, knitting, religious activities, studying, playing chess, embroidery work.

Taghi Azad Armaki, and Gheasvan (2003), in their study 'Sociology Survey of Cultural Changes in Iran', found out the important values in life, such as family, friends, spare time, politics, work, and so on. Among them, the following values are more important; family: religion, work, helping others, friends, spare time, and politics.

The researcher has done a detailed study of some families to find out the recreation pattern of women in Tonekabon city.

1. Mrs Mirdar is 32 years old and she lives in the area of Shohada. She is a teacher. Most of her recreation pattern include resting, going to parties, reading magazines, playing with her child at home, and watching TV at night with her husband.

2. Mrs. Saadat, 19 years old, is a housewife and she got her diploma certificate. She lives in the area of Tonekabon Mohal. She got married recently and she mainly spends her recreation time at home resting, watching T.V and reading women's magazines.

It is obvious from the case study that respondents have modern recreation patterns such as; going to parties, reading magazines, watching TV and traditional recreation pattern such as; playing with her child at home and resting.

With regard to the above-mentioned, we can observe that in the data of recreation pattern, women had participation in both modern and traditional level. Modern pattern included; reading newspaper, magazine, listening to radio, chess, sewing, knitting, embroidery works, studying, visiting, attending parties, visiting clubs and the tradition pattern included, visiting neighbours, recreation with children, attending religious activities and resting.

## III. PERSONAL HABITS

The important means of personal habits are food/ nutrition, hygiene, house, sleep, work, clothes, and smoking. According to Mohammad Sharbatian, (2000), in his *'Comparative Study of the Students of Art'*, stated: personal habits are one of the most important cultural, healthy, and hygiene dimensions in our society. Consideration to these values is important in family cultural structure. It means that people from the initial of life, had special consideration to cultural and social training. Englewood Cliffs, Prentice- Hall, (1960:73) stated that "health has an important effect on both the amount of leisure available to the people and the quality of its enjoyment. Satisfying use of leisure cannot substitute for poor health, lost family and friend, or an inadequate pension. Nor can it take the place of the feelings of usefulness and purposefulness which are probably the greatest needs of the aged".

P. Bourdieu (1979) stated, Tastes for food also depended on the idea each class has of the body and of the effects of food on the body, that is, on its strength, health and beauty; and on the categories it uses to evaluate these effects, some of which may be important for one class which may rank it in very different ways. Thus, whereas the working classes are more attentive to the strength of the (male) boy than his shape, and tend to go for products that are both cheap and nutritious, the professions prefer products that are tasty, health-giving, light and not fattening. Taste, a class culture turned into nature, that is, embodied, helps to shape the class body.

In order to understand personal habits of the respondents the following questions were asked. "What do you think about choosing food?" Majority of the respondents around 96% said that choosing food is important and only 3% of them answered it is not important.

The next question put to the respondents was "How do

you decorate your food?" More than 45% of the respondents explained that they like "simple decoration". While nearly 21.3% said they decorated food "according to mood" and about (27.8%) respondents said they decorated food 'according to other people". Lostly, just (5.8%) of the respondents revealed that decorating food is "not important" for them.

Next question was "What is your habit in eating". Among the respondents above 46.2% declared that they have "fixed time" to eat food and nearly 33.2% of them answered "depended on the days". While around 20.6% of the respondents announced that there is "no difference" for them.

The next question put to the respondents was "who gives weekly menu?" Almost 44.8% of the respondents said weekly menu was arranged by "wife". And approximately 39.7% answered it was arranged by "husband". But nearly 39.7% revealed that food table was arranged by both of them.

The respondents were asked the following question "How often do you eat food outside?" Almost half of the respondents announced that they go outside for eating food "once a month". Some of them said they go outside for eating between "twice a month" and "once a week".

The next question was "What kind of food material is used in a week". Most of the respondents revealed that they consume mixed food nutrients such as; proteins, vitamins, and calcium.

The next question was about "The significance of food items in a week" such as: rice, pulses, oil, milk, vegetables, and non-vegetable. All respondents declared that they use all food items weekly.

The last question put to the respondents was "What is your taste?" Almost more than half of the respondents announced that their taste is oily food.

It is clear that data demonstrate that the majority of the respondents like to make food, decorate food and eat it at regular or fixed times. Some of the respondents go to restaurants at least once a month. The respondents stated that they use proteins, vitamins, calcium in their daily meals and they use rice, oil, milk, vegetables, meat, eggs, and fish. It seems that most of the respondents have an awareness of the importance of eating nutritious food and balanced diet.

In a group interview, five respondents living in the area of Paskelaye said that personal habits are of great importance; especially regarding food and nutrition. Those who had small children believed that daily food must include the needed vitamins and proteins for children.

In a group interview, ten respondents living in the area of Azadi said that food is very important for their husbands. The food must be delicious and different foods must be cooked every day such as meat and chicken. Along with the food, there must be salad, vegetables, pickles and olives. Such things are important for the women because the satisfaction of their husbands and children is important to them.

In the group interview another respondent was Mrs. Rostamkalayee, living in Arian area. She was a professor who was 45 years old. According to her, personal habits were very important. Hence, during holidays or at weekends she tried to do her best to make a good meal for her husband and her baby.

In a group interview two other respondents said that personal habits and giving importance to daily meals were necessary; as the saying goes "the way to a man's heart is through his stomach". In different seasons they cook different foods; for example, during winter they cook fish.

It is clear from data of group interview; respondents said that personal habits were of great importance especially regarding food and nutrition. Also they believed that daily food must include the needed vitamins and proteins for children. They said that, they preferred cooking special food like fish and meat during the holidays.

## IV. HYGIENE

The next question put to the respondents was "hygiene": "what is your idea about taking a daily bath, cosmetic, nose and face plastic surgery, hair cutting, body management". And "How often do you visit a beauty parlour?"

**Table 3.11 : Hygiene**

| *Body management* | *Very necessary* | | *Necessary* | | *Less necessary* | | *Not necessary* | | *Total* |
|---|---|---|---|---|---|---|---|---|---|
| | *Freq.* | *%* | *Freq.* | *%* | *Freq.* | *%* | *Freq.* | *%* | |
| Daily bath | 184 | 40.4 | 78 | 17.1 | 66 | 14.5 | 128 | 28.1 | 456 |
| Cosmetic in body | 92 | 20.3 | 112 | 24.7 | 131 | 28.9 | 118 | 26.0 | 453 |
| Plastic surgery | 32 | 7.0 | 75 | 16.5 | 144 | 31.7 | 203 | 44.7 | 454 |
| Face plastic | 19 | 4.2 | 44 | 9.7 | 116 | 25.7 | 273 | 60.4 | 452 |
| Hair cutting | 64 | 14.1 | 188 | 41.4 | 98 | 21.6 | 104 | 22.9 | 454 |

Above fifteen respondents replied all factors for body management are important and younger generation believed that it is very important. Almost 99% of the respondents said they had visited beauty parlour, and among them half of the respondents said they have visited beauty parlour once a month. Besides, 43% percentage said they like normal make up, only 17.8% said that they like heavy make up, others went for medium.

Next question was "Do you make up at home"? If no then why?" Around 68.5% of the respondents answered "yes". While nearly 31% said "no", out of these more than 77% of the respondents declared "we don't like it" and nearly 22.9% of them said "we are old".

It is clear from the data majority that of the respondents take care of personal hygiene such as taking daily bath, using cosmetics, and having hair cut. Most of the respondents said that they visited beauty parlour each month. In addition to this the present study shows that most of the women, living in the research location, used a means of body management, like nose plastic surgery and heavy make-up especially among the young ladies either at home or in society.

Azadarmaki and Chavoshian (2003), in their research *'The Human Body as a Medium of Identity'*,about 'body management in life' found out in all items of body management such as nose and face plastic surgery, make up, hair cutting, and use of perfume and so on. People in high social class payed more attention to their body. Therefore social class is important in body management. Moreover, there is relation between education and body management.

Nejaba Behzadizn, (2004), in her study *'Beauty and Culture'*, states modern technology has be come an impurtant aspect of life. It has also influenced beauty such as facial surgery.

In the group interview, two of the students believed that personal hygiene was very important. They believed that plastic surgery for beauty is accepted and good. According to them make-up, especially for girls, is of great importance because it adds to the beauty of the face.

In the group interview, ten teachers' respondents said that personal hygiene was very important and crucial. But putting of make-up must depend on the place, the time and the situation. According to them putting make-up is not accepted every where.

In the group interview with three doctors, they pointed out that personal hygiene and plastic surgery for the sake of beauty are something natural. According to today's progress in technology and science of medicine, it is okay.

In the group interview seven of the respondents who were employees at a university said that at official places such as a university they are not allowed to put on make-up. But they liked make-up and they used cosmetics at home and not at official places.

In the group interview five respondents, who were housewives, liked cosmetics but they put on make up differently at different places. For instance, they put on make up freely at home, and they may go to extremes but they make a balance in public places.

It is clear from the data of group interview study, that most of the women, living in the research localities, used a means of body management especially in the younger age like nose plastic surgeary and heavy make up either at home or in the society. Nowadays with regards to progress of technology and science the lifestyle of women in body management has greatly changed.

## V. HOUSE

N. Anderson (1961) stated, the home is the place where family members do most of their television viewing, reading, indulging in hobbies and general relaxing. Most social contact with relatives and friends occurs in the context of the home. Although it would be an exaggeration to say that the spending of leisure at home is new, it has certainly grown in comparison with the past. Parker (1976) said, to day the average home has become a more inviting place in which to spend leisure time. The higher standard of living has enabled improvements to be made in the size, appearance and furnishing of many (though by no means all) homes. The home furnishing industries with their high-pressure advertising and the home-beautiful magazines have played their part in this process, which has also been helped by relevant school courses and other educational efforts.

Mohammad Hasan Sharbatian, (2000) in his *'Comparative Study of the Students of Art'*, stated: one of the cultural index life modes is residential space which reveals cultural similarity and differences among families and social groups in society. Having good residential space and welfare possibilities and comfort, have been cultural dimension of life mode.

Elyasi, Mahzad (2004) in her study *"Girls' Cultural Anthropology Survey'* said the space inside and outside of house has influence on people's lifestyle.

To understand the respondent's lifestyle and level of recreation at home, the following questions were asked: "What is your favourite work when you are at home? How do you decorate your home? And what is your criterion in choosing home furniture?"

Answering these questions most of the respondents declared that when they are at home, their favourites are studying, watching T.V., talking with family members, and nearly 47% answered to all above-mentioned factors. Moreover, respondents declared that they like simple and beautiful decoration and furniture at home.

Next question was, "Who works at home?" nearly half of the respondents answered: 'wife and husband' and 35.1% answered only 'wife' also 8.8% said 'servant' and 2.5% respondents said husband works at home.

To find out about the question "Do you think educated women will spend more time in the society or at home?" Nearly (82.8%) of the respondents said they spend their time both "at home and in the society".

In the present study, both traditional and modern houses have been seen. In modern houses, everything such as furniture, carpet, colour, and decoration are set and are the latest mode. But in traditional houses everything is simple and old and related to traditions.

In the group interview, five of the respondents said that decoration of the house depends on the financial state of the people. One of the respondents, who was a housewife and her husband was a farmer, said that it was not affordable for her to decorate her house as doctors or engineers do.

In the group interview, ten of the respondents said that the decoration of the house is important for them. There must be a harmony among the colours used for decorating the house; and, the furniture must be that of the high class.

In the group interview, six of the respondents said that they decorated their houses according to the models and the new styles shown on satellite T.V. or in magazines.

In the group interview four of the respondents said that decoration of the house depended entirely on the salary of the husband and the wife. If a person is well paid, accordingly (s) he can decorate his/her house better.

It is clear in the group interview that attitude of women to lifestyle in house is changing. In modern house, every thing such as furniture, carpet, a harmony among the colours and decoration are set and are selected among the latest modes.

## VI. SLEEP

Our bodies grow and develop from the first moments of life; they provide us with a living, physical basis for our identity where all aspects are literally embodied. So in the life cycle, sleeping plays role for every person to balance body and mind/emotions.

As we know, sleeping is necessity for each and every person; and, also, in the present research, people had different sleeping time according to their job.

To understand the respondents sleeping habit the following question was asked: "What is your habit in sleeping?"

To this question, nearly 29.8% of the respondents answered they have "fixed sleep time" and around 38.8% of them answered "depended on the days" Almost 31.9% of the respondents said there is "no difference" for them as far as sleep time is concerned. Also above half of them said that they like to sleep in "silence". Moreover, 18% of the respondents answered they "study" before sleep, and 21.6% declared they "listen to music".

Finding out habits concerning the time of sleeping, more than half of them said they sleep between "9pm- 10 pm" they sleep soon because they want to wake up early in the morning. Nearly 49.8% of the respondents answered they sleep between "11pm- 12pm". They sleep late, because they study, and they have insomnia."

And about the question "What time do you wake up? Around 40.1% of the respondents said that they wake up before 6 am. And above 58% declared that they wake up after 6:30am.

Most people under study feel that sleeping is necessary for each and every person; and it depends on the nature of their jobs, so some of them have to get up early in the morning and like to sleep in silence. And few of the respondents have fixed sleeping time.

Fakouhi and Ansari (2002) in their study, '*Time and Cultural Personality Formation in Two Girls' High School in the City of Tehran*' when they asked "How they spend leisure time" the respondents replied at home they have leisure such as rest, sleep.

The researcher has done a detailed study of some families to find out sleeping habits of women in Tonekabon city.

One of the families was Mrs. Rahmani's family. She is 30 years old; living in the area of Shirud. She said that "sleeping" depended on the daily work and habits of people. But the husband of Mrs. Rahmani sometimes worked during the nights. So, his time of sleeping depended on his job.

Mrs. Hoseini, who is a nurse living in the area of Arian, said that three times a week she had to be in the hospital during the night. So her time of sleeping depended on her job.

Mrs. Ahmadi, who is a doctor living in the area of Azadi, is 42 years old and she said that there is no regular, fixed time to sleep for them because they must be in the hospital constantly.

It is clear in case study the respondents' habits of sleeping time depended on their daily works and jobs.

## VII. WORK

Parker, (1976:65) writes about leisure and work, 'in some ways leisure is bound with work. It is easy to think of leisure as opposite of work, or to define it as time left over after work. But the relationship between these two spheres of life goes much deeper than that. Not all human societies have made the same distinction between leisure and work in the modern industrial world. As compared with other times in history and other parts of the world, leisure and work today show certain broad features and trends. Work influences leisure in many ways and some observers believe the opposite influence is becoming more apparent. There are various theories which have recently been developed to explain the different possible types of relationship between work and leisure'. Parker stated in modern society, we find three broad approaches to leisure and work. One (which is clearly declining) is in the religious tradition mentioned above; work perceived as the serious business of life and leisure as subsidiary or even non- existent. The second approach represents a complete swing of the pendulum: Leisure seen as an aim of life, and work as merely a mean to that end. Thirdly, we have the beginning of a more integrated approach to both leisure and work, appreciating them as reconcilable parts of a whole, each able to enrich the other, like the craftsman or artist.

In order to understand the respondents, daily work time, the following questions were asked: "what is your daily habit about work time, how many hours a day you work and what is your idea about work time". Almost 83.3% said work time is "regular", 16.7% of the respondents answered "irregular". Above half of them said "8 hours", other work time was between "4-6 hours" a day. Above 53% of the respondents said we have "sufficient" work time, and 15.8% said it is "too much" and at last 31.2% said work time is "average".

To find out about the question, "What is your idea about women's ability comparied to men", about 48.4% of the respondents said, 'it is the same', and 26.4% answered 'men's ability is more than women's'. And for the idea 'Women's ability is more than men', few respondents 14.8% agreed. The next question was "Are you satisfied with your wages?" and "if no why?" The answers were, 48.2% 'yes' and 51.8% 'no'. Respondents said that they are not satisfied because the cost of living is more than their income.

It is clear from the data that the attitude of the respondents toward their work influences leisure in many ways. The respondents under study have regular work time. They believed work for women is very important, especially out of home; however, women have free time inside the home.

Bagher Sariukhani, and Maryam Rafatja, (2004), in their study *"Sociological Factors Related to the Re-divination of Women's Social Identity"*, pointed out: The result indicate that the structural position of women as compared with the personal sense of identity has greater influence in redefining women's social identity and their capacity to resist stereotypical gender definitions. Additionally, the study indicates that the impact of education has been greater than the impact of employment on the redefinition of women's social identity. Religious women, who have attained higher education, experience a lack of cohesion in their identity. However, as these women continue with their education, they begin to rethink their religious and traditional identities, and as a result are able to greatly overcome the contradictions. Moreover, the study shows that the religious women due to impact of education have been more eager to tradition function such as housework.

Zahra Elmi, (2003), in her study *'Macro-Economic Policies and the Labor Market for Women in Iran'*, declared that: The present Iranian labour market is faced with a huge number of people who are seeking work and with insufficient growth of job opportunities, it will entail increasing rate of unemployment. The process of job creation has neither met the demands of the unemployed, nor those of university graduates, and the country's population as a whole. In this study, a review will be made of the major economic policies at the macro level with their impacts on women's work force in the labour market. Policies such as reducing fertility rate, expansion of education, controlling inflation rate, privatization, and economic growth were analyzed in this study. The finding indicated that, economic growth improves macroeconomic capacities, but unemployment rate is reduced slightly.

Alireza Amini, (2003), in his study *"Gender Approach to Imbalance in the Labour Market"* explained: The aim of the study is to identify indicators that demonstrate the lack of gender balance in the Iranian labour market. The findings point to the low level of women's participation, despite the increase in their presence as compared with the past decade, as well as the concentration of women in relatively few economic activities. The result also point to the relatively higher level of unemployment among women, especially young women in urban areas, as compared with men's unemployment level. The gender-based employment indicators in different parts of the country speak of alarming gender imbalances. In urban areas, the problems of women's unemployment and in rural areas the high rate of male unemployment exist at alarming levels.

## VIII. CLOTHES

The set of questions, were about clothes, understanding their clothing patterns and the following important factors they consider while buying clothes fashion, beauty, quality, comfort, and uniqueness were asked to the respondents.

**Table 3.12: Clothes**

| *Clothe Patterns* | *Very important* | | *Important* | | *Average* | | *Not important* | | *Total* |
|---|---|---|---|---|---|---|---|---|---|
| | *Freq.* | *%* | *Freq.* | *%* | *Freq.* | *%* | *Freq.* | *%* | |
| Fashion | 51 | 14.6 | 86 | 25.4 | 133 | 38.0 | 77 | 22.0 | 350 |
| Beauty | 149 | 32.7 | 184 | 40.4 | 77 | 16.9 | 46 | 10.1 | 456 |
| Quality | 204 | 44.6 | 188 | 41.1 | 48 | 10.5 | 17 | 3.7 | 457 |
| Comfort | 225 | 49.3 | 182 | 39.9 | 42 | 9.2 | 7 | 1.5 | 456 |
| Uniqueness | 135 | 30.0 | 145 | 32.2 | 110 | 24.4 | 60 | 13.3 | 450 |

A majority 88% of the respondents said fashion, beauty, quality, comfort and uniqueness are important for them in buying clothes. Only 22% said the above factors are not important for them.

The next question put to the respondents was "Do you like western, modern, and traditional clothes?" and "if yes or no why?"

Nearly half of the respondents said 'yes' and 'we like western and modern clothes' because they have 'variety,' 'better colour', 'better design'. Also, above half of them answered 'they don't like western' clothes, and they like simple and traditional clothes because these clothes show their culture and identity.

The next question was "Do you like traditional clothes?" More than 72.7% of the respondents like traditional clothes, "because traditional clothes show our culture, history and tradition." While few respondents said they didn't like traditional clothes. The traditional clothes include scarf, shirt, *shalith* (a short creased skirt), vest, skirt, pant and *shaol* (wrapped around the waist).

Traditional Iranian clothing has its roots extending back at least as far as thousands of years ago. Today, neither young girls residing in the provincial towns, nor the ones living at rural areas are any more interested in putting on their traditional garments.

Most of the new generations feel that western clothes look fine, and convenient for every day wear, for formal and family occasions and functions.

When it came to buying clothes, most of the respondents believed that fashion, beauty, quality, comfort and uniqueness are important for them. Most of the new generations feel that western clothes look fine and convenient for everyday wear, for formal and family occasions and functions. Also nearly half of the respondents said that they liked western and modern clothes because of their variety, better colour and better design. Some of them like a traditional clothes which includes scarf, shirt, shalith (a short ceased skirt) vest, skirt, pants and shawl wrapped around their waist.

Fakouhi and Parsapajo (2002) in their study *"Formation of Culture Identity Among Teenage Girls of Islamabad, Karaj"*, says girls choose clothes according to their social and cultural situation. Nowadays, they choose clothes with regard to mode as shown in shop-window. Of course school and college clothes are different from party and street clothes.

Mohammad Sharbatian, (2000), in his study *"A Comparative Study of the Lifestyle of the Students of Art, Boys of 18 to 25 years old in Cultural Centre of Bahman and Amir Kabir"*, finds out: In various social class, preference of cloth using, cloth price, satisfaction to cloth are different. Therefore, any person used clothes according to his family position and social and economic situation.

Parvin Sasgarnejad, (2002), in her investigation on *University Professors and Traditional Businessmen,* states taste is very important in both groups to buying and choosing clothes. Of course in different social level, (upper, middle and low) income also has important role.

In a group interview, five respondents living in Azadi area said that they preferred simple, neat, tidy clothes which are of a good quality.

In a group interview, seven respondents who were students said that clothes must be of different colours and beautiful. Some of them preferred clothes of modern style.

In a group interview, ten respondents said that wearing clothes depended on whether the person is in a good shape or not. They also believed that it depended on the personal interests of people.

In a group interview, eight of the respondents who were housewives, living in the area of Paskelaye, said that the clothes they used at home are different from those they wear at parties or formal occasions. They also believed that there is a difference between the way young people and old people dress.

In a group interview, twelve of the respondents believed that buying clothes depended on the financial problems of the people.

Above data of group interview shows that, most participants reported that, they found fashion, quality, comfort and uniqueness as important for buying clothes. And in younger women under study they like more western clothes and wear modern clothes. And of course different socio-economic conditions and income have an important role in buying clothes.

## IX. SMOKING HABITS

The last question put to the respondents was, "Do you smoke?" Above 95% of the respondents replied 'no', because it is not good for health. And some of the respondents said 'yes' for relaxation, and recreation; they feel it is mode of modern lifestyle, and some said: it is just a habit, you feel you need to keep it, a habit with no pleasure and no use.

A mens the women under study, majority respondents, did not smoke. And few of them said that they used to smoke for relaxation, recreation, to have fun, and they felt it was a mode of modern lifestyle. It is that in Iran, especially in research, study of women with modernity and some modes in both old and new generation didn't like to smoke.

Fakouhi and Ansari (2000) in their study *"Leisure Time and Cultural Personality Formation in Two Girls' High School in the City of Tehran"* declare that people think time of leisure is timing for wasting their time in street or to prowl (to hang round) or going somewhere without any plan. Also it is either time to visit boyfriend, for smoking, drinking and watching movie.

## X. ACCESS TO INFORMATION AND MASS MEDIA

Today's mass media are the products of highly developed technologically-oriented states. The media of mass communication is significantly relevant to lifestyle, leisure time activities. People more exposed to mass media are expected to be more modernized, because these media of mass communication transmit new ideas and ideologies to the people exposed.

The important means of mass media are newspaper, magazines, periodicals, radio, television and internet. Felipe Korzenny, Stella Ting, Toomey (1992:256) said: "It is important, however, to distinguish between the instruments technology provides and their actual use by human beings. As a result we should avoid automatically transferring the already uncertain social effectiveness or positive of mass media and technology to leaders or individuals who use them for their own purposes. Only if the complex interrelationships between media, cultures, individuals, ideologies, and states can be better understood, will we be able to make mass media no dominant, efficient, effective partners in the evolution of new, mutually accepted processes of interaction." Therefore, Sharare Mahdizade, (2001), in her study *'Survey in T.V and Innovation'* said according to innovation and modernization process and changes in modern world, mass media has an important role in people's lifestyle and leisure time. Therefore, the T.V. program should be useful for leisure time. In the present study, the respondents were asked the following question, "Do you read newspapers/magazines/periodicals?" "Which and where do you take?" "Do you listen to radio/watch television?" "Do you use internet?"

A majority 82.1% of the respondents said that they read newspapers. Out of these, 30.1% read newspaper daily, while 38.7% sometimes and near 11.4% said that they read rarely. Nearly 17.9% said that they never read newspapers because they were illiterate; but, they discussed various topics with their friends and family.

Answering the question "which news do you read in the newspaper?", respondents clarified that they read any news, such as; news related to Iran, international news, political, women's news, cultural, art and sport news. Most of them were interested in reading "news related to Iran" and less interested in reading "sport news".

The next question put to the respondents was "Where do you get the newspaper"? The respondents are provided with the newspaper through purchasing, library, subscription, and other sources. Among them more than 60.6% said they obtain newspaper through purchasing.

The next question put to the respondents was "what magazine do you read"? The respondents are provided with a list of different types of magazines: family magazine, political, social, film, women's. Almost 60% answered "family magazine" and other respondents went for the other items.

When researcher asked them 'where do you get the magazine', most of the respondents said that they get their magazine from stalls and on subscription. Less among them replied they get through friends, neighbours and library.

The next question was; "What do you read in the magazine?" Nine alternative response categories were provided to them. These categories were: stories, poems, sports, article, political, social news, economic and current topics. Among the respondents 24.4% answered they read "stories of the magazine". And around 16.6% said they read "current topic". Meanwhile, respondents to other items were nearly 12%.

Next question put to the respondents was "Do you listen to the radio programs". Around 80% of the respondents said they listen to the radio. And almost up to 97% watch T.V/ movie. Out of these 77% said that they watched T.V and movies "any time" and above 52% "once a week". While nearly 19.9% of the respondents said they never listen to the radio and less than 2% of them didn't watch T.V/movies.

The question "What radio program do you listen to?" Had eight alternative response categories: classical songs, news, talks, sports, drama, films songs, hygiene, social, and all of them. So around 20.1% like to listen to "classical songs" and 21.4% respondents liked to listen to "talks" and nearly 27.6% of the respondents were eager to listen to "all of the programs?" Meanwhile the other items had very less percentages.

The next question was, "Do you use internet". Above 53.6% of respondents said "yes" and around (46.4% ) answered "no". The answer 'if yes or no, then what for?' For "if yes" the answers were "knowledge, chatting, fun, for getting information and all of them". And answer "if no" they said "because there is no facility, no time, and some of them said we don't know how to work with internet. The above data shows that majority of the women used important means of mass media such as newspaper, radio, and T.V, internet, for awareness and obtaining information at national and international level. Also more than half of the respondents were familiar with new technology such as internet.

The information obtained from the respondents is about their exposure to various media of mass communication like films, radio, newspapers, magazines, journals, T.V and internet. Data also indicated that majority of respondents listened to radio, and nearly 97% watch T.V/movie. The majority of respondents read newspapers and magazines, such as international news, political, women's news, cultural, art and sport news, stories, poems, articles, social news, economic and current topics.

Regarding, their exposure to internet, more than half of the women under study were familiar with new technology such the as internet. And new generation used internet more in leisure time, specially for chatting.

Fakuohi and Mirdamadi (2003), in their study '*Cyberspace*

*as Urban Space in Tehran'*, stated; today oral/linguistic communication and use of language is the most important tool in internet. Necessity of oral/linguistic communication is patience and persistence and in this matter women have more abilities. People use this technology both in leisure time and working time. Also he added 'That persons connect to internet with their own income (self financial), shows the importance of this medium in daily life'.

Sharare Mahdizade, (2001), in her study *'Survey in T.V and Innovation'*, said according to innovation and modernization process and changes in modern world, mass media have an important role in people's lifestyle and leisure time. Therefore T.V. programs should be useful for leisure time.

In a group interview, thirteen respondents living in Shohada area said that today mass media plays an important role in getting information about the country and the world. The respondents said that nowadays there has been a great impact of radio, T. V. on the masses because those who saw T.V. were exposed to all programmes such as educational, recreational, sports, news, etc. Women read magazines about women, especially the magazine named *"Today's Women"*.

In a group interview of seventeen respondents living in the area of Azadi and Khoban Razga, they said that they liked reading magazines and newspapers about women. They also watched all the family and social TV serials. They also are interested in listening to radio programs which are about family hygiene.

There fore from the above research data it shows that most of the Tonekabon women living in the research localities use important means of mass media such as newspaper, magazine, radio, T.V. and internet for awareness and information of national and international events.

## Conclusion

According to present study, the respondents stated that most of the women spent their leisure time according to traditional pattern such as; visiting the park, public library, celebrating festivals, museum, historical places, and social work, as well as modern pattern of spending leisure time such as; gym, body building clubs, cinema, museum, concert hall, exhibition, tourist place, voyage, restaurant, fast food restaurant, coffee shops and social work. Many young respondents clearly spent lots of time in modern pattern of leisure time activities. So we can observe both traditional and modern pattern of spending leisure time. In sum there is a change in the lifestyle as for as leisure time activities are concerned and there is also continuity in some respect.

Among other traditional forms of leisure; the case study found that respondents also spent leisure as follows: going out or visiting neighbours, going to religious cities, watching TV and listening to radio, visiting parent's family and some times with in-law's family. [And also spend their leisure time in modern pattern such as; going to fast food joints or restaurants, visiting exhibitions, tourist places, and chatting.]

In this study about the recreation pattern, the majority of the respondents attend parties and visit neighbours. Also some of them spent their leisure time by chatting online with people, visiting clubs and visiting different organizations, and skin clinic.

In family recreation, most of the respondents were interested in visiting their relatives and organizing games at home. Furthermore, this research shows that women were eager to listen to the radio, read newspaper or magazine and play with children.

The research revealed that most of the respondents preferred to take rest. There were of course varying degrees of rest, incumbent to the nature of work performed by then. And, they also participated in other activities such as sewing, knitting, religious activities, studying, playing chess, embroidery work. Moreover, we observe that the data revealed a mixture of both traditional and modern recreation reflective of changing lifestyle. In modern pattern including; reading newspaper, magazine, listening to radio, chess, sewing, knitting, embroidery works, studying, attending parties, visiting clubs and the traditional pattern including, visiting neighbours, recreation with children, attending religious activities and resting.

Majority of the respondents under study like to make food, decorate food and eat it at regular or fixed times. Some of the respondents go to restaurants at least once a month. The respondents stated that they use protein, vitamins, and calcium in their daily meals through the use of rice, oil, milk, vegetables, meat, eggs, and fish. It seems that most of the respondents have an awareness of the importance of eating nutritious food and balanced diet.

The sample group interviewed in the present study revealed that personal habits are of great importance, especially regarding food and nutrition. Also they believed that daily food must include the needed vitamins and proteins for children. They said that they prefeced cooking special food like fish and meat during the holidays.

Furthermore, majority of the respondents take care of personal hygiene such as taking daily bath, using cosmetics, and having hair cut. Most of the respondents said that they visited beauty parlour each month. In addition to this the present study shows that most of the women, living in the research location, used a means of body management, like nose plastic surgery and heavy make-up especially among the young ladies either at home or in society.

The group interview surgery that most of the women, living in the research localities, used a means of body management especially in the younger age like nose plastic suargery and heavy make-up either at home or in the society. Nowadays, with regards to progress of technology and science, the lifestyle of women in body management has greatly changed.

This study has cast light upon both traditional and modern house. In modern houses everything such as furniture, carpet, colour, and decoration are set and are the latest mode. But in traditional houses everything is simple and old and related to traditions.

Moreover the group interview shows that women's attitude toward lifestyle in house is changing. In modern house every thing such as furniture, carpet, a harmony among the colours and decoration are set and are selected according to the latest trends.

Most of the women under study feel that sleeping is necessary for each and every person; and it depends on their nature of jobs so some of them have to get up early in the morning and like to sleep in silence. And few of the respondents said they have fixed sleeping time.

It is clear from the case study that the respondents' habits of sleeping time depended on their daily work and jobs.

In the present study, the attitude of the respondents toward work influences leisure in many ways. The respondents under study stated that work time is regular. They believed work for women is very important, especially out of home; however, women have free time inside the home.

Iranian traditional garment have their origin in the ancient history of Persia; however, today, neither young girls residing in the provincial towns, nor the ones living at rural areas are any more interested in putting on their traditional garments. Wearing clothes has became another rapidly changing facet of life in Iran.

Most of the new generations feel that western clothes look fine, and convenient for every day wear, for formal and family occasions and functions.

When it came to buying clothes, most of the respondents believed that fashion, beauty, quality, comfort and uniqueness were important for them. Most of the new generations feel that western clothes look fine and convenient for everyday wear, for formal and family occasions and functions. Nearly half of the respondents preferred modern or western clothes, due to their variety, better design or colours, etc, but, some of them liked traditional clothes which included scarf, shirt, *shalith* (a short creased skirt) vest, skirt, pants and shawl wrapped around their waist.

In addition, the present group interview shows that most participants reported that they found fashion, quality, comfort and uniqueness as important for buying clothes. And alwing younger women under study, they liked more western clothes and wearly modern clothes. And of course in different socio-economic conditions income has an important role.

Regarding smoking, the majority of women under study, said that they did not smoke. And few of them said that they smoked for relaxation, recreation, to have fun, they feel it is mode of modern lifestyle. In Iran, both modern and semi-modern women alike, especially in research area, didn't like to smoke.

Besides, nowadays mass media are the products of highly developed technologically-oriented states. There is a strong impact of urbanization and modernisation on the women under study. As a result, in the location of study, the information obtained from the respondents about their exposure to various media of mass communication like films, radio, newspapers, magazines, journals, T.V and internet. Data also indicated that majority of respondents listened to radio, and nearly 97% watched T.V/movie. The majority of respondent read to newspapers and magazine, such as international news, political, women's news, cultural, art and sport's news, stories, poems, article, social news, economic and current topics.

Regarding their exposure to internet, more than half of women under study were familiar with new technology such as internet. And new generation used internet more in leisure time specially with on-line chatting.

# 4

# Socio-economic, Educational Life and Political Participation

In the previous chapter, we have discussed lifestyle and leisure time activity of women. The present chapter concentrates on socio-economic life, educational life and political participation of women in Tonekabon city.

This chapter is divided into four sections. The first section deals with the socio-economic life. The second section concentrates on their attitudes toward education. Third section focuses on their attitude toward occupation. The fourth section deals with the political participation of Iranian women.

Actually, in Iranian society the current economic, social and political situation, have called upon women to play new functions that are basically different from what their condition in a traditional and underdeveloped social system would warrant. Yet what has created a crisis in the area of women's legal rights is the inequality that exists in the process of development and certain approaches to the question of development. On the other hand, while the legal system has its roots in the period of traditionalism, the economic, social and cultural qualities of society are undergoing a process of transformation. Consequently, the legal system is no longer capable of responding to the needs of this transitioning period of political, economic, social and cultural reality. In all societies for the majority of people, productive activity, or work, occupies a major part of their lives more than any one other type of activity.

## I. ATTITUDE TOWARDS SOCIO-ECONOMIC LIFE

In the traditional joint family, social life of women was restricted to family and relatives. Also only place for holiday, leisure, amusement and entertainment was family. The sexes' segregation was accomplished in a variety of ways. The spheres of work for men and women were distinguished and marked. The spheres of work for women were "looking after the household work" and men usually worked outside.

In the pre-modern society, women were usually restricted to home. And generally they had established relations with close-families and neighbours belonging to their own community and religion. But in the modern world due to influence of modernization, it has been observed that the sphere of women's work gradually expanded from home to social activities relationships.

Economy is one of the most important aspects of society. It is for the production, distribution and consumption of goods, both essential and non-essential. Thus, the economy is indispensable as far as the survival of a society is concerned.

To support this idea Long and Kobert; (1978:320) stated: 'Economic relationships are embedded in social and cultural relationship.'

Amit Kumar Gupta (1986:38) says: "the economic setting is regarded by many experts as the "social field" which overwhelmingly determines women's status and roles. Family structure and concomitant domestic cycle phases are other variables which are affected by the economic setting and in turn influence societal attitudes relating to the status of women. The relationship between the economic setting, family structure and the status of women throws a number of important considerations into relief."

Economic pressures had been the main reason for employment irrespective of the nature of family. The working women with single member family were mostly in employment because of economic pressures.

From the anthropological point of view, economics is the comparative study of the relations between the system of allocation and management of the resources of societies of various types and structure and the values of that society.

In this section, in order to find out the role of women in the social activities, the question 'visiting friend, parties, were asked:

On finding about women under 'visiting friend', almost 90% of respondents said they have been visiting friends. Only 10% said they have not visited their friends. The majority of respondents 88% said 'yes we go to parties', and nearly 12% answered that they did not participate in parties with friends.

To understand the attitudes towards social life of the respondents, the following questions were asked: "How can women be empowered?" The respondents have suggested different ways to empower women such as: by education, by economic independence,by bringing more women in politics, equal rights for both genders in all respect, by bringing a fundamental change in the prevailing mindset, by role fluidity, by having a strong voice in decision making process and by recognizing them as productive members of society.

But majorities 48.6% of respondents feel that by 'education' and by 'equal rights for both genders in all respect', women can be empowered.

Jaleh Shaditalab, (2004) in the research "Rural Women's Bank of Hesarbone", the outcome of a participatory approach said; 'Empowerment perspective is based on the experience of the developing countries' organizations dealing with women's issues. It envisages the alteration of the structures and conditions which impose inequality on women. Considering the fact that inequalities differ in different parts of the world according to historical, cultural and social conditions, the approach is based on the assumptions:

(1) improving women's self-reliance will increase their power;

(2) power is not the sign of an individual over the other' but is the right to choose and influence the choice;

(3) the objective is to control the material and non-material resources which contribute to fair distribution and equality.'

She said the empowerment approach is similar in one aspect to the welfare. It acknowledges women's reproductive role and provision services for its improvement. However, it emphasizes women's other two roles as well: participants in the labour market, and society's decision-making structure. It also holds that by raising consciousness, women themselves fight oppression.

The next question was "What is your opinion on the legislation giving equal rights to women in father's/husband's property"? Nearly 99.8% of respondents said they 'agreed' and when researcher asked them 'why' they answered "because we should not differentiate between the genders so that 'equal right' is important for women." Another question the researcher raised was "Does women's employment influence the power structure of family?" and "why"? Almost 99.5% of the respondents said that 'yes' job is important because, it makes 'family stability' and helps 'family economy'. The next question was "Do you feel that educated women are better mothers?" and "why"? Around 98.9% of the respondents said 'yes', because education increases direct and indirect costs and moreover increase the economical benefits. Education increase women's personal and social awareness too. Education will change the people's approaches, values, and beliefs and also encourages them to family planning and birth-control. Also educated women bear fewer children, who have better chances of surviving infancy, of being healthy, and of attending school. When women are adequately educated, everyone benefits.

And about this question "What is your opinion about women being portrayed as commodities in cinema/ advertisements?" whether she should accept it then or if she should reject it then and "why"? About 81% of the respondents said that she should reject it, because women are not like goods and this portrayal of women is not acceptable in our culture. And 19% of respondents said that they should accept it because they believed that women also can participate in any job and this, also, is a kind of job for women.

The next question put to the respondents was "what is your opinion about T.V serials on the family?" The respondents laid more stress on traditional image of woman. The woman is shown as a shadow of her husband. Such serials curb the women's mental and intellectual growth. Nearly 39.2% of respondents revealed that the women are shown as slaves of their families, and 18.4% of them said that such T.V. serials harm women's personality. Also around 21.2% of respondents replied that it is not showing the role of women in the real life.

In the present study, the women's attitudes toward social life show that women are empowered. They have importance for education and economic independence. The majority believed, by education and by equal right for both gender in all respects, women can be empowered.

Majority of the respondents said they have been visiting friends regularly and some times they go to parties.

As regards the reasons of taking up employment, it influences the family power structure. On the whole, the respondents took up jobs mainly due to economic reasons. With education women are having fewer children, have better chances of surviving infancy, of being healthy, and of attending school.

Most of the respondents believed that women should reject being portrayed as commodities in cinema/ advertisements. They said women's position is very high in their culture.

In the present study, majority of respondents said that T.V. serials laid mores stress on traditional image of women. Most of the time women are shown as powerless and weak members of the family and they should be just obedient to their husband and they have not any role in family decision making but this is opposed to reality.

## II. ATTITUDE TOWARD EDUCATION

Education has many advantages. Evidence shows that the education of girls and women increases income, productivity, individuality, economic development, besides welfare and so on. Also, education authorizes women, preparing them with increased independence in every realm of their life.

Education has been seen as the magic wand for curing the ills of society. The developing countries placed great emphasis on it and hoped that expansion of education would also bring about greater equality in their societies. One of the most important economic and social changes in recent decades which had very important consequences to population was the development of universal education, in general and women's education, in particular. On the other hand, education is the most important way to change the approaches. Education will change the people's approaches, values, and believes and also encourages them to family planning and birth-control. Education also provides women to find better job opportunities and associate them with economic growth. Therefore those countries that have more educated people in the labour-force would lead to greater maintenance of the growth.

According to statistical survey, nearly half of the population of Iran are women; so that women are also counted as half of the labour-force. And this labour-force is called 'human capital', and if they are educated, they could be of more benefit for the country. Obviously, the education and addition of new individuals to the labour-force leads to economic growth. When women are sufficiently educated, everyone benefits in the society. There is the strong link between a woman's education and her employment and income.

In order to understand attitudes towards education, the following questions were put to them. "What is your opinion about equal opportunity for both women and men in education field?" If 'yes' or 'no' then why? Almost 92% of the respondents replied 'yes', they believed that equal opportunity for both women and men in education is important, because gender is not an advantage and both genders have the same ability and talent. And only 8% answered 'no' there are not equal opportunities for women and men regarding education, because education for men is more important than women, since he is supposed to find a good job by higher education; and moreover, men should manage the life and family.

The next question they were asked: "Did you get an equale opportunity in terms of education as compared to your brother?" if 'yes' or 'no' then why? Around 81.4% of the respondents replied 'yes', they had equal opportunity in terms of education as compared to their brother because, with education they will find better job, independence and good opportunity of marriage. And nearly 18.6% of the respondents said 'no' they hadn't equal opportunity in terms of education as compared to their brother because their family believed education is not necessary for girls, they should be at home and look after children and family. Moreover education for girls makes them independent and it poses problems in future common life and they added to their families' economic problems. Above all, boys should take care of parents especially in old age. And at last, education for boys is important because they will get a better job.

The frequency of 'equal opportunity' is cross-tabulated against the level of education, income and occupation, of the respondents, the results of cross- tabulations shows that an equal opportunity in terms of education gets more in highly educated family. Furthermore the table reveals that women from families with high "income" and high "occupation" have more equal opportunity for girls in terms of education.

To the question "Is higher education more important for a boy than a girl?" Nearly 32.8% of the respondents said higher education is more important for a boy than a girl and

27.6% said education for boy and girl is of equal importance. And more than 39.6% answered education is less important for a boy than a girl.

This question of the frequency of 'higher education more important for a boy than a girl' is cross tabulated against the level of education, income and occupations of the respondents. The results of cross tabulations show that in lower income and low occupation and less-educated family 32.8% education for boys is more important than for girls. Furthermore the data reveals that women from families with lower income, education and occupation 27.6% have stated that 'Education for boy and girl is equal'. In less education, income and occupation items the table shows that in 39.6% 'Education is less important for a boy than girl'. We can say that there is difference of opinion regarding the importance of each boy and girl among lower income and educated families.

The next question put to the respondents was "How do you evaluate women's education? Why?" Almost (95%) of the respondents said, education for women is 'very important' because education improves and expands women's thoughts and activities in the personal life and the society, and also 5% answered women's education is 'not important' because they will at last be at home and look after the children and the family. (Onafterthought: It underscores the attitude that girls among the traditional sample group may never fully use their education.)

Women Studies Centre, Iran (2002) reported that women constitute half of the population (49.25%) in Iranian society. The major parts of them have professional status and higher education. And nowadays more than 65% of people admitted to universities are women. But in recent years, the rate of women's unemployment with higher education reaches up to 21%.

When they were asked "Does women's education influence the status of power in family? and if 'yes' or 'no' then why?" Most of the respondents 93.7% said 'yes', women's education influences the status of power in the family, because women can participate in social work; and furthermore, if women go for higher education, everyone would be benefited. When a woman follows a career, she can help the family with the extra money. It is generally known that children whose mothers have a job are more independent. The financial independence of women leads to independence of mind, self-confidence and decision-making. Above 6.3% of the respondents said 'no' women's education does not influence the status of power in the family, because "money" brings power not "education", and women's power would not be increased just with education.

Shamsosadat Zahedi, in her study *Women's Resources are Wasted in Iran (1996)*, stated that only 8% of all Iranian women were employed outside the home. Neither are the figures encouraging for women with higher education. In 1996 statistics shows that only 38% of women with university degrees had work. The public sector is the main employer for educated women. And 87% of working women are public employees. When you look at the top managerial level, only 5% are women. In private sector there are only few women. She also thinks that it must be very discouraging for female students to observe the high number of unemployed educated women.

In the present study respondents stated that education is necessary and significant for both women and men and education opportunity must be equal for both of them. Furthermore they explained that the ability and aptitude of both genders is the same. Actually educated women have more influence on their life and they can increase family income, happiness, and social welfare.

Whereas education has significant role in family and educated women could find better job, thus education and employment have positive role in family stability. Moreover they believed that job makes them financially independent and powerful.

Majeed Movahed, Halimeh Enayat and Abbas Gorgi (2005) in "The Impact of Socio-Economic Factors on Women's

Attitude Towards Gender Inequality" in Iran said that there is a significant relationship between independent variables such as women's education, women's income, father's and mother's education, husband's income, education of parents and mother's employment status and dependent variable such as gender inequality. The results also indicate that the most important variables are women's education, mother's education, employment status for gender equality.

The researcher has done a detailed study of some families to find out the attitude toward education of women in Tonekabon city.

1. Mrs Karimi, 38 years old, a professor, living in Karim Abad area, is the wife of a dentist. She says that today education is necessary for everybody. Fortunately, today, women in comparison to men are more interested in studying. She believes that education is equally important for both men and women. A good father and mother who are educated can improve the quality of their lives. She says: "I teach at university. I love my job. I have peace in my life. So, although I work out, it does not hurt my family. My husband is a dentist and he supports us very well but I think financial independence is necessary for women."

2. Mrs Mehrabi, an employee, 34 years old, lives in Shohada area and her husband is a business man. She has a son. She says that education is a crucial thing for a woman. She found a job with her diploma certificate and she worked for ten years. But later she decided to go to university so she entered university. Now that she has higher education, she has more happiness. Although her husband does not have academic education, he did not prevent his wife to educate herself.

3. Mrs. Amiri, 39 years old, living in Tonekabon Mahal, is a judge. She says that education must be compulsory for women because women who are educated can change their lives. In comparison with women who lived before the Islamic Revolution, today's women are more active and have higher education. According to her, education does not belong to

working women only; a housewife needs to be educated as well.

4. Mrs Hoseini, 53 years old, is a housewife and lives in the area of Goleijan. She says that education is the best thing for women. She can only read but she has always loved education. Her father was old-fashioned and did not let her study but she tried hard to educate her children and to send them to university. She has four children and all of them are university graduates.

It is clear from the case study that respondents believed that education is essential for both gender in the same way. An educated parent can improve the quality of their lives. Nowadays women in Iran are more educated and they are active in politics and social activities.

## III. ATTITUDE TOWARD OCCUPATION

This section has focused on attitude toward occupation of women in Tonekabon city:

Occupational status and income levels are interrelated. Causes that prompt women to enter into employment are as complex as those influencing other choices that affect their way of life. It is generally believed that socio-cultural changes play a very important role in creating a situation in which women would like to seek employment. While one would not deny the importance of socio-cultural changes, there are several other factors which lead one to take individual decision to work or not to work. It might be that in a particular cultural context, one was in a position to get employment but her desire might not be translated into action, if she was not in a position to go out of home.

Therefore to understand the respondents' attitude toward occupation the following question was asked "How do you feel about women having a job?" Why? Above 98% of the respondents said job for women is 'important' because job makes women financially independent and helps the family economy. And nearly 2% said job for women is not important, because after marriage their husband will support them and she should do home duty.

And the other question was "What were your parent's aspirations for you in terms of job?" Above 33% of the respondents said, 'their parents encouraged them to enter in teaching profession' and 6.5% answered 'their parents like them to take a government job and nearly 20% said their parents wanted their children to become a physician, an engineer or a lawyer'. Above 26.7% of the respondents stated that they wanted to continue family occupation and nearly 13.3% said they like to get married and settle down as a house wife.

The other question was; "Should both men and women involve in earning money?" A majority (96.3%) of the respondents said both men and women should involve in earning money and only 3.7% said it is not important.

And the next question was "How do you think about urban women's activities comparing with the rural women?" Why? Almost 93.9% of the respondents said urban women have more activities because 'in cities there are more facilities such as government jobs, private companies, business and so on. And nearly 6.1% said in rural areas also there are lots of activities for women such as handicrafts art, agriculture, animal husbandry, etc.

The last question was "Which one is more satisfactory, being a house wife or working outside for income?" more than 60.2% of the respondents said they are satisfied with working at home as housekeeper instead of working outside for wage (income) and 17% said they are satisfied while working outside for income the same as working at home as housekeeper. And 22.8% answered they are more satisfied with working outside for income instead of being house keeper.

The above data show that the majority of respondents believed that job makes women financially independent and improves family income. Also they stated urban women have more activities than the rural women, because in cities there are more facilities.

Hosein Mirzai (2002), in his study "Factors Impacting Iranian Women's Economic Participation", said that recently, the most important reasons for the presence of women in work places have been: first, the level of education. Second, motivation and interest for financial independence and third, migration from villages to cities.

To understand the attitude towards the economic life of the respondents, the following questions were asked: "Do you feel that there are disadvantages of having an employment? If yes or no, then how?"

Majority (75.7%) of the respondents said, 'Yes' there are disadvantages of an employment and they gave different reasons of disadvantage of employment, such as: if they go to work, they haven't enough time for their husband and children and

(1) there would not be leisure time to pursue your hobbies,

(2) they can't attend social functions in the family,

(3) once married, you are burdened with dual duties, and

(4) male colleagues make advances and you have to handle them. Some (24.3%) of respondents said no, there is no disadvantage of an employment because social work raises the human thought.

Tagh Azad Armaki, and Gholamreza Ghaffari (2004), in their study about "Generational Attitudes toward women," said: The survey on the attitudes of Iranians towards women's employment reflects changes in the ratios of 'agree' to 'disagree'. About 30years ago, 30% of the people in urban areas agreed to women's employment outside the domestic spheres. Whereas in 1995, more than 50% agreed with female's employment (Abdi and Goudarzi 1999:30). However, the ratio of the agreed to the disagreed people is about 1% for men, and about 1.9% for women.

The next question put to the respondents was "What

type of occupation would you suggest for women and wives? Why?" More than half (56.6%) of the respondents feel that teaching is a good occupation for women and wives because this job is more respectable and it provides them with more leisure time and holiday. In Iran, there are three months holiday for schools in summer and during all festivals schools are closed. Moreover, school timing is morning or afternoon so that teachers have more free time and they can do their home duties too. Although, the salary is not quite enough but they have suggested because it isn't hard or boring. Few (9.7%) of the respondents' interest was in banking occupation because of salary, social position and facility that banks give them such as; financial support, loan for buying home, car, etc. Some (13.3%) suggested being a "physician." They explained that attitude of the society towards physicians is very good and they have high income and they don't need government job and can establish a clinic and work there. Even nowadays, with lots of people graduated from Medical schools or Colleges, yet the need for the specialist physician is more. And some 20.4% of the respondents stated that they are just looking for a job and it is not important what it might be, because job opportunities in Iran are very limited.

In Iran, one of the significant social changes is the emergence of families with two income sources, both husband and wife. This type of family, despite benefiting from a blending of roles, is faced with certain pressures, which stem from traditional division of labour within the family and new responsibilities of its members. If the conflict is not properly managed, it has a negative impact on the social unity and function of the family as well as the emotional and social health of the members. When asked to them: "How do you spend your salary?" More than half of the respondents (58.8%) said they contribute to the family income for every day life. Also some 10.6% of the respondents explained that, they will save salary to improve their life situation such as buying home, car, property and so on. While few (9.7%) of the respondents stated that they spend part of the salary for personal works such as buying ornaments and everything they like. Some of them (13.6%) said they spend the whole salary as they want and these groups of women include two parts: first, those women whose husbands had good job position and they din'nt need their wives' salary and the second group of women explained that they are working so that salary is for themselves and they should spend as they like. And few (3.8%) said they gave some parts of their salary to their parents. Among this group of women some said their husbands know about their support to parents and the others said this is personal matter and they pay from their own salary and there is no need to say to their husbands. The other respondents stated they give all the salary to their husband because they believe that it would be spent for common life.

The next question put to the respondents was: "Do you suffer disadvantages in the office on account of your sex?" if 'yes' or 'no' why? Nearly 42.2% of the respondents said 'yes' because 'men do not accept women in senior positions'. Further, they explained that men always like to have key posts and they think women are unable to do great works or they don't want to accept a woman to be as their boss or superior to them. More than 57% of the respondents mentioned that they are not suffering disadvantages of gender because it depends on persons and their attitude to gender. Respondents feel that women are as powerful as men. Women should not accept that differentiation of gender makes them unable and they should show their abilities. Taghi Azad Armaki, Gholamreza Ghaffari (2004), in their study about "Generational Attitudes toward women", said: 'Attitudes towards gender constitute one of the important socio-cultural characteristics of all communities. It is used as the criteria to distinguish communities as male/female-oriented, or traditional/modern. In addition, changes of attitudes towards women are indicators of the realization of changes in social, cultural, political and economic aspects of the societies. There is no doubt that the attitudes affect and induce changes in all the action, processes and social structures at micro, mezzo and macro levels. As a result, attitudes towards women, in general, can explain the situation of other social and cultural aspects of any society'.

It was found that when researcher asked "Have you succeeded in establishing a balance between the house and office?" and how? Nearly 46.7% of the respondents stated they have fully maintained balance between house and job having regular time table and helps of relative or others. This group of women stated their husband and parents have important role in this matter. Men, like women, work at home and take care of children and also maybe their parents help them to look after children, so that everything is with agreement both of men and women. Also, they send their kids to kindergarten or school in school bus or private car. As a result, they hadn't any problem to make balance between home and office, because their husbands know women work outside the same as men and share their income with family. Above 49% said they also have partial balance with regular time table and other's help. This group said because their husband are not cooperative with them and they should do home duty alone. Moreover, they have nuclear family and their parents are living in another city or living separately so that they couldn't make a full balance between home and office. And near to 3.45% of the respondents said that they are struggling to balance the house and office work because their husbands are not cooperative at all. Actually, they explained that their husbands disagree with their job and say that women should just work at home and look after their children.

In addition, of business persons, clerks, teachers, physicians, engineers, lawyers, university teachers, government officers, university students, researcher asked "Are you satisfied with your present job?" and 'if no, why'? Most of them (86.3%) were satisfied with their job and were totally happy and pleased. Some (13.3%) said they were not satisfied with their job. Because they had less income.

And the next question was, "does financial independence result from women's employment?" most of the respondents (85%) said 'yes', financial independence results from women's employment and only a few (15%) answered 'no'. The other question was "To what extent financial independence influences women's decision making?" Majority of the respondents (85.6%) believed that financial independence has a great impact. Because of financial independence women can involve in family decision making; even sometimes they are more powerful than their husbands. A few (9.2%) of them stated because they are unemployed and their husband is working and has income so they take decision and women haven't any role in family decision making. And very few (4.8%) of them stated because they are unemployed and they have no role in decision making.

The next question was "What is the main reason for your working?" Nearly half of the respondents (46.6%) said because they want to contribute for the family income and help family economy and provide for better amenities for their family and children. Some (27.6%) of them stated because they want to make use of their education and talent and believe that women should work like men and use their ability to help the family and society progress. Some (13.8%) of them believed that jobs make them economically independent and they can be autonomous in society. Moreover, nearly (6.9%) of the respondents explained that, because they want to improve their social status. And a few (3.8%) of them said they want to help their parents because they have economic problems and the others said they liked working places to get away from monotony and boredom of housework.

Safi and Emadzadeh (2003), in their study "The Impact of Economic Factors on Women's Employment in Iran", believe that the number of the employed women in Iran compared with other developing countries is less. But they expect a sudden rise within two decades.

When the researcher asked last question "Are the financial

independence and women's employment important for family?" if 'yes' or 'no' then why? Most of the respondents (96%) said 'yes' financial independence and women's employment is very important for the family. Because their income helps the family welfare and women feel calm. With the present economic situation in Iranian society and the high cost of living, it is difficult for men to provide the family with all necessities. Moreover, women's employment makes them calm and it changes their attitude towards the society. Only a few(4%) answered 'no' because it is men's duty to provide for family with facilities and women's duty is to provide a peaceful space at home and take care of the husband and children.

A large number of the respondents replied that there are some disadvantages also when women are employed. Because when they are working out side, they will not have enough time to look after children because they are busy and tired. Also they have not enough time for their husband.

In the present study more than half of the respondents stated that teaching is a good job, because teacher is good and superior among the people. Also there is more free time to be at home and do their responsibility to the family. And some of the women were interested in other occupations such as: banking, being a physician or government officer due to better financial support and income and social statur.

Majority of the respondents believed that financial independence has a great impact. Because of financial independence women can be involved in family decision making: even sometimes they are more powerful than their husbands, and their income helps the family welfare and women feel calm. With the present economic situation of Iranian society with the high cost of living, it is difficult for men to provide the family with all necessities.

In the present study the women who had jobs talked about salary, they contribute to the family income for daily expenditure and some persons spent part of the salary for personal desite such as buying ornaments and everything they like. And other idea was that they give some parts of their salary to their parents. Almost all women belonging to different occupations such as clerks, business persons, teachers, physicians, engineers, lawyers, university teachers, government officers, university students were satisfied with their job and were totally happy and pleased.

The respondents stated that sometimes they suffer disadvantages in the offices because of their gender. They added that is difficult for men to agree with women being in senior positions or boss. Because they think women are unable to do great work. Perhaps this is due to women's emotional nature.

About their idea on economic inpact, they stated that their work could help the family income and it improves family economic situation. Therefore, they can provide more facility for family growth and progress.

Most of the respondents replied that women should be given higher education in all branches of knowledge. They also believed education was important like employment in economic independence. Additionally, the power structure of patriarchy within families, women's greater awareness, their social participation, employment and education, will transform their status, the family, and society.

In the research "Factors in the women's engagement in economic activities in Iran", by Mirzadeh (2003), it shows that the rise in the education level, income earning and financial independence can be considered as the most important factors in the contribution of women in the recent years. Further he says that the importance of women's social status would lead to major changes in social and economic variables in the country. The rise in the number of women in the socio- economic struchure of the country after the Islamic Revolution, a change in the views to women co-operating in different sectors, have contributed to develping the foundations for their presence. The rate of the women's contribution in the work market would change in different stages of the process of development. In the very initial stages, agricultural activities attract lots of effort. Since to work in the fields and gardens, one does not need to be a skilled professional, women participate in such activities along with men. Therefore generally speaking, women's contribution in the productive activities is much more than other field. Migrating from villages to the towns and cities and the female migrants being almost uneducated is also a cause for women's lesser contribution in the work market.

In order to study the effect of education, occupation, income and age of the respondents in the participation of their socio-economic activities, these variables were cross-tabulated against the respondents' socio-economic activities such as: visiting friends, parties and empowerment, women's jobs, influence of family.

**Table 4.1: Age and Visiting Friends**

| *Age in Year* | *Often* | | *Some time* | | *Mostly* | | *Never* | | *Total* |
|---|---|---|---|---|---|---|---|---|---|
| | *Freq.* | *%* | *Freq.* | *%* | *Freq.* | *%* | *Freq.* | *%* | |
| 16-24 | 42 | 39.6 | 30 | 28.3 | 2 | 1.9 | 32 | 30.2 | 106 |
| 25-34 | 36 | 45.6 | 33 | 41.8 | 2 | 2.5 | 8 | 10.1 | 79 |
| 35-44 | 36 | 35.6 | 58 | 57.4 | 1 | 1.0 | 6 | 5.9 | 101 |
| 45-54 | 20 | 36.4 | 28 | 50.9 | 2 | 3.6 | 5 | 9.1 | 55 |
| **Total** | **134** | **39.3** | **149** | **43.7** | **7** | **2.1** | **51** | **15.0** | **341** |

**Table 4.2: Marital Status and Visiting Friends**

| *Marital Status* | *Often* | | *Rarely* | | *Never* | | *Always* | | *Total* |
|---|---|---|---|---|---|---|---|---|---|
| | *Freq.* | % | *Freq.* | % | *Freq.* | % | *Freq.* | % | |
| Unmarried | 38 | 34.2 | 37 | 33.3 | 4 | 3.6 | 32 | 28.8 | 111 |
| Married | 87 | 44.8 | 90 | 46.4 | 2 | 1.0 | 15 | 7.7 | 194 |
| Divorce | 0 | .0 | 8 | 80.0 | 1 | 10.0 | 1 | 10.0 | 10 |
| Widow | 0 | .0 | 12 | 92.3 | 0 | .0 | 1 | 7.7 | 13 |
| **Total** | **125** | **38.1** | **147** | **44.8** | **7** | **2.1** | **49** | **14.9** | **328** |

**Table 4.3 : Education and Visiting Friends**

| *Education* | *Often* | | *Rarely* | | *Never* | | *Always* | | *Total* |
|---|---|---|---|---|---|---|---|---|---|
| | *Freq.* | % | *Freq.* | % | *Freq.* | % | *Freq.* | % | |
| Illiterate | 2 | 18.2 | 9 | 81.8 | 0 | .0 | 0 | .0 | 11 |
| Primary | 3 | 33.3 | 5 | 55.6 | 0 | .0 | 1 | 11.1 | 9 |
| Secondary | 8 | 32.0 | 12 | 48.0 | 2 | 8.0 | 3 | 12.0 | 25 |
| Diploma | 43 | 40.6 | 45 | 42.5 | 3 | 2.8 | 15 | 14.2 | 106 |
| Graduation and above | 79 | 42.2 | 76 | 40.6 | 2 | 1.1 | 30 | 16.0 | 187 |
| **Total** | **135** | **39.9** | **147** | **43.5** | **7** | **2.1** | **49** | **14.5** | **338** |

**Table 4.4: Occupation and Visiting Friends**

| *Occupation* | *Often* | | *Rarely* | | *Never* | | *Always* | | *Total* |
|---|---|---|---|---|---|---|---|---|---|
| | *Freq.* | % | *Freq.* | % | *Freq.* | % | *Freq.* | % | |
| Unemployed | 24 | 35.3 | 38 | 55.9 | 2 | 2.9 | 4 | 5.9 | 68 |
| self employed, clerk, business women | 27 | 38.6 | 28 | 40.0 | 1 | 1.4 | 14 | 20.0 | 70 |
| Students | 17 | 38.6 | 5 | 11.4 | 1 | 2.3 | 21 | 47.7 | 44 |
| teacher, principle, govt. officer | 57 | 47.5 | 52 | 43.3 | 2 | 1.7 | 9 | 7.5 | 120 |
| Doctor, engineer, lawyer, professor | 11 | 30.6 | 23 | 63.9 | 1 | 2.8 | 1 | 2.8 | 36 |
| **Total** | **136** | **40.2** | **146** | **43.2** | **7** | **2.1** | **49** | **14.5** | **338** |

Table 4.5: Income and Visiting Friends

| Income | Often | | Rarely | | Never | | Always | | Total |
|---|---|---|---|---|---|---|---|---|---|
| | Freq. | % | Freq. | % | Freq. | % | Freq. | % | |
| Unemployed | 24 | 35.3 | 38 | 55.9 | 2 | 2.9 | 4 | 5.9 | 68 |
| No income | 42 | 36.2 | 46 | 39.7 | 2 | 1.7 | 26 | 22.4 | 116 |
| Below1000 | 17 | 43.6 | 15 | 38.5 | 1 | 2.6 | 6 | 15.4 | 39 |
| 1001-3000 | 44 | 44.9 | 43 | 43.9 | 2 | 2.0 | 9 | 9.2 | 98 |
| 3001-6000 | 19 | 46.3 | 19 | 46.3 | 2 | 4.9 | 1 | 2.4 | 41 |
| 6001 and above | 9 | 28.1 | 22 | 68.8 | 0 | .0 | 1 | 3.1 | 32 |
| **Total** | **131** | **40.2** | **145** | **44.5** | **7** | **2.1** | **43** | **13.2** | **326** |

Table 4.6: Age and Go to Picnics or Parties

| Age in Year | Often | | Rarely | | Never | | Always | | Total |
|---|---|---|---|---|---|---|---|---|---|
| | Freq. | % | Freq. | % | Freq. | % | Freq. | % | |
| 16-24 | 50 | 34.2 | 66 | 45.2 | 17 | 11.6 | 13 | 8.9 | 146 |
| 25-34 | 33 | 33.7 | 49 | 50.0 | 11 | 11.2 | 5 | 5.1 | 98 |
| 35-44 | 44 | 34.6 | 66 | 52.0 | 13 | 10.2 | 4 | 3.1 | 127 |
| 45-54 | 18 | 27.7 | 32 | 49.2 | 12 | 18.5 | 3 | 4.6 | 65 |
| 55above | 1 | 100.0 | 0 | .0 | 0 | .0 | 0 | .0 | 1 |
| **Total** | **146** | **33.4** | **213** | **48.7** | **53** | **12.1** | **25** | **5.7** | **437** |

Table 4.7: Marital Status and Go to Picnics or Parties

| Marital Status | Often | | Rarely | | Never | | Always | | Total |
|---|---|---|---|---|---|---|---|---|---|
| | Freq. | % | Freq. | % | Freq. | % | Freq. | % | |
| Unmarried | 46 | 31.5 | 69 | 47.3 | 18 | 12.3 | 13 | 8.9 | 146 |
| Married | 92 | 36.7 | 116 | 46.2 | 30 | 12.0 | 13 | 5.2 | 251 |
| Divorce | 2 | 14.3 | 11 | 78.6 | 0 | .0 | 1 | 7.1 | 14 |
| Widow | 2 | 15.4 | 7 | 53.8 | 4 | 30.8 | 0 | .0 | 13 |
| **Total** | **142** | **33.5** | **203** | **47.9** | **52** | **12.3** | **27** | **6.4** | **424** |

Table 4.8: Education and Go to Picnics or Parties

| *Education* | *Often* | | *Rarely* | | *Never* | | *Always* | | *Total* |
|---|---|---|---|---|---|---|---|---|---|
| | *Freq.* | *%* | *Freq.* | *%* | *Freq.* | *%* | *Freq.* | *%* | |
| Illiterate | 0 | .0 | 8 | 61.5 | 4 | 30.8 | 1 | 7.7 | 13 |
| Primary | 18 | 39.1 | 18 | 39.1 | 4 | 8.7 | 6 | 13.0 | 46 |
| Secondary | 6 | 20.7 | 11 | 37.9 | 8 | 27.6 | 4 | 13.8 | 29 |
| Diploma | 28 | 26.2 | 52 | 48.6 | 23 | 21.5 | 4 | 3.7 | 107 |
| Graduation and above | 83 | 37.2 | 118 | 52.9 | 14 | 6.3 | 8 | 3.6 | 223 |
| Total | 135 | 32.3 | 207 | 49.5 | 53 | 12.7 | 23 | 5.5 | 418 |

Table 4.9: Occupation and Go to Picnics or Parties

| *Occupation* | *Often* | | *Rarely* | | *Never* | | *Always* | | *Total* |
|---|---|---|---|---|---|---|---|---|---|
| | *Freq.* | *%* | *Freq.* | *%* | *Freq.* | *%* | *Freq.* | *%* | *Freq.* |
| Unemployed | 20 | 24.7 | 38 | 46.9 | 20 | 24.7 | 3 | 3.7 | 81 |
| Self employed, clerk, business women | 36 | 35.3 | 41 | 40.2 | 15 | 14.7 | 10 | 9.8 | 102 |
| Students | 14 | 31.8 | 24 | 54.5 | 4 | 9.1 | 2 | 4.5 | 44 |
| teacher, principle, govt. officer | 43 | 34.4 | 66 | 52.8 | 12 | 9.6 | 4 | 3.2 | 125 |
| Doctor, engineer, lawyer, professor | 35 | 43.8 | 36 | 45.0 | 2 | 2.5 | 7 | 8.8 | 80 |
| Total | 148 | 34.3 | 205 | 47.5 | 53 | 12.3 | 26 | 6.0 | 432 |

Table 4.10: Income and Go to Picnics or Parties

| *Income* | *Often* | | *Rarely* | | *Never* | | *Always* | | *Total* |
|---|---|---|---|---|---|---|---|---|---|
| | *Freq.* | *%* | *Freq.* | *%* | *Freq.* | *%* | *Freq.* | *%* | |
| No income | 38 | 27.0 | 70 | 49.6 | 25 | 17.7 | 8 | 5.7 | 141 |
| Below1000 | 15 | 30.0 | 17 | 34.0 | 13 | 26.0 | 5 | 10.0 | 50 |
| 1001-3000 | 33 | 32.0 | 57 | 55.3 | 9 | 8.7 | 4 | 3.9 | 103 |
| 3001-6000 | 17 | 32.7 | 32 | 61.5 | 1 | 1.9 | 2 | 3.8 | 52 |
| 6001 and above | 38 | 46.9 | 33 | 40.7 | 2 | 2.5 | 8 | 9.9 | 81 |
| Total | 141 | 33.0 | 209 | 48.9 | 50 | 11.7 | 27 | 6.3 | 427 |

**Table 4.11: Age and Do Women Jobs Influence the Power Structure of Family**

| *Age in Year* | *Yes* | | *No* | | *Total* |
|---|---|---|---|---|---|
| | *Freq.* | *%* | *Freq.* | *%* | *Freq.* |
| 16-24 | 133 | 100.0 | 0 | .0 | 133 |
| 25-34 | 90 | 98.9 | 1 | 1.1 | 91 |
| 35-44 | 114 | 100.0 | 0 | .0 | 114 |
| 45-54 | 56 | 98.2 | 1 | 1.8 | 57 |
| 55 above | 1 | 100.0 | 0 | .0 | 1 |
| Total | 394 | 99.5 | 2 | .5 | 396 |

**Table 4.12: Marital status and Do Women Jobs Influence the Power Structure of Family**

| *Marital status* | *Yes* | | *No* | | *Total* |
|---|---|---|---|---|---|
| | *Freq.* | *%* | *Freq.* | *%* | *Freq.* |
| Unmarried | 130 | 100.0 | 0 | .0 | 130 |
| Married | 231 | 99.1 | 2 | .9 | 233 |
| Divorce | 10 | 100.0 | 0 | .0 | 10 |
| Widow | 10 | 100.0 | 0 | .0 | 10 |
| Total | 381 | 99.5 | 2 | .5 | 383 |

**Table 4.13: Education and Do Women Jobs Influence the Power Structure of Family**

| *Education* | *Yes* | | *No* | | *Total* |
|---|---|---|---|---|---|
| | *Freq.* | *%* | *Freq.* | *%* | *Freq.* |
| 1 | 2 | 3 | 4 | 5 | 6 |
| Illiterate | 12 | 100.0 | 0 | .0 | 12 |
| Primary | 35 | 97.2 | 1 | 2.8 | 36 |
| Secondary | 29 | 100.0 | 0 | .0 | 29 |
| Diploma | 101 | 99.0 | 1 | 1.0 | 102 |
| Graduation and above | 201 | 100.0 | 0 | .0 | 201 |
| Total | 378 | 99.5 | 2 | .5 | 380 |

**Table 4.14: Occupation and Do Women Jobs Influence the Power Structure of Family**

| *Occupation* | *Yes* | | *No* | | *Total* |
|---|---|---|---|---|---|
| | *Freq.* | *%* | *Freq.* | *%* | *Freq.* |
| Unemployed | 74 | 97.4 | 2 | 2.6 | 76 |
| Self employed, clerk, business women | 89 | 100.0 | 0 | .0 | 89 |
| Students | 37 | 100.0 | 0 | .0 | 37 |
| Teacher, principle, govt. officer | 113 | 100.0 | 0 | .0 | 113 |
| Doctor, engineer, lawyer, professor | 74 | 100.0 | 0 | .0 | 74 |
| Total | 387 | 99.5 | 2 | .5 | 389 |

**Table 4.15: Income and Do Women Jobs Influence in Power Structure of Family**

| *Income* | *Yes* | | *No* | | *Total* |
|---|---|---|---|---|---|
| | *Freq.* | *%* | *Freq.* | *%* | *Freq.* |
| No income | 125 | 99.2 | 1 | .8 | 126 |
| Below1000 | 49 | 100.0 | 0 | .0 | 49 |
| 1001-3000 | 96 | 100.0 | 0 | .0 | 96 |
| 3001-6000 | 46 | 100.0 | 0 | .0 | 46 |
| 6001 and above | 68 | 100.0 | 0 | .0 | 68 |
| Total | 384 | 99.7 | 1 | .3 | 385 |

The results of the cross-tabulations show that educated women are better mothers. Attainments of the younger age are high. Also, it was found that in these factors "visiting friends and parties," married women had participated more than unmarried women. Moreover, women with high education and high occupation had participated more.

The researcher has done a detailed study of some families to find out the socio-economic activities women in Tonekabon city.

1. Mrs. Mohamadi, living in Arian and 32 years old, has completed her B.A. degree in psychology. Regarding social participation, she said every person has some social activities like visiting friends at home or at work. She believes that educated women can have a better social participation and power in society. Educated women can find better jobs. In comparison to women who lived before the Islamic Revolution, today's women are more active.

2. Mrs Rostampour, 41 years old and living in Azadi area, says that women can freely be active in society nowadays. Education helped women to be more active in various aspects in society.

It is obvious from the case study that respondents participate in social activities every day like visiting friends at home or at work. Moreover they explain that educated women can have a better social participation and power in society.

## IV. POLITICAL PARTICIPATION OF WOMEN

This section has focused on political participation of women in Tonekabon city.

JENA (1993:149) stated "Modernization is basically a summarizing concept, which includes several dimensions in its fold. Besides technological and socio-cultural changes, it also addresses to the nature of political participation, which would be an indicator of the growth of modernization in a particular society. In the traditional societies political system and its governance was the privilege of the few. Political authority was linked up with charisma and divine will and, therefore, unquestionable. With the change and development taking place in other sub-systems of the society, political sub-system, the nature of its functioning and the process of legitimising have undergone a series of transformation. The contemporary political system, whether monarchy, military dictatorship, party dictatorship, parliamentary or presidential form of government, cannot thrive without the support of the people at large. Political modernization does not discriminate participation of the people on the basis of the caste, religion, language, ethnicity, class and sexes. Therefore, with the picking up of the modernization process in Europe, political participation of women was considered as "inevitable."

Myron Weiner (1971:164) said "the concept of political participation refers to any voluntary action, successful organized or unorganized, episodic or continuous, employing legitimate or illegitimate methods, intended to influence the choice of public policies, the administration of public affairs, or the choice of political leaders at any level of government, local or national.

"Women's participation in politics is essential to their advancement: without their voice being heard at the decision-making level, how will women get the changes they need in employment, health, education and access to supportive services? On the other hand, without such changes, without equal access and opportunity, how are women to get into power?"

Amit Kumar, (1986) stated that, in modern society, where decision-making is a collective process, political persons have tremendous significance. Political Power helps political one to impose one's will on the others. In a democratic society, political activity is a process of authoritative allocation of values in a society; this includes voting, contesting elections, campaigning, party activism, etc. There might be formal as well as informal channels through which the political power is exercised. As far as women are concerned, we can define political power as the degree of equality and freedom enjoyed by women in the shaping and sharing of power and the value attached to this role by society. Further, women's participation at the grassroots level has also to be assessed.

To understand the respondent's level of political participation and their attitude towards politics the following questions were asked:

"Do you participate in the activities such as canvassing, agitations, political meeting, and hunger-strikes"? Above 15.4% of the respondents said 'yes', they always participate in political canvassing. While 71.9% of the respondents said that they some times participate in the canvassing. Only 12.7% of the respondents said that they never participated in canvassing. And for "participation in the agitation," nearly 7.8% of the respondents said that they have always participated in the agitations, while, 8.9% said that they have some times participated in the agitations. And majority 83.2% of the respondents said they have never participated in the agitations. When researcher asked them about political meetings, above 4.7% of the respondents answered yes, they participate in political meeting regularly and a few (8.3%) said some time they participate in political meetings. Most of the respondents (87%) said they have never participated in political meetings. Lastly, about participation in hunger-strikes, majority (62%) of the respondents said yes they attend to hunger-strikes and also (11.7%) of the respondents said some times they have attended hunger-strikes. Nearly 26.3% of them answered no, they did not attend hunger-strikes.

Voting is the most important and basic means by which citizens are assimilated in the political process and learn the art of exercising of power.

To find out how many percent of the women participate in voting, the question put to them was "Do you vote?" Among the respondents above 68.1% replied that they participate in voting regularly. And nearly 19% of them said they participate in voting some time. Also, around 12.9% of the respondents answered they did not participate in voting.

To understand the criteria of vote, researcher asked them "What are the criteria in choosing a candidate when they vote?" the answers were such as, education, political experience, crime-free record, party manifesto, caste/religion. Among the respondents more than 65% believed that, education, political experience, crime-free record, party manifesto, caste/religion are the most important ones. And nearly 35% of the respondents said all the factors are less important.

And to the question "Do you discuss politics with your families, friends, relatives, etc?" Nearly (46.2%) of the respondents mentioned that yes, they have discussed it with families, friends, relatives and around (53.8%) of them said no, they didn't discuss it with anybody.

To find out "What is the role of women in politics?" nearly 11% of the respondents stated that since half of the population of Iran are women, the role of women in politics is more important. And about 29.3% of them answered that the role of women is important, and most of the respondents (45.9%) said that the role of women in politics is low, and lastly 13.8% of them said that women's role in political issues is very low.

M. Shiroudi (2005), in his research entitled "Women's Socio-political Role in the Modern Iranian Society", makes a comparison between women's contribution in the social-political activities in the Mashroute period, before the Islamic Revolution and after that. He categorizes different views into three groups, as follows:

1. The number of the women who played a role in different historical period of the country and even to day is not worth mentioning at all.
2. Some believe that women are influential in the modern history of the country, but it has always been secular, anti-religion ones.
3. The most significant role in the last hundred years, has been played by Muslim women and not those who were living in the palaces, and secular antireligion ones. But, since they could not publish or announce their words, it has been faded. According to the social history of women in Iran, Muslim women were so influential in the social changes. In order to guard the religion and the country, following the religious leaders, women participated in the anti-colonization, anti-regime, and anti-dictatorship movements. They improved their contribution in the socio-political movements making

> use of their experience till 1979 Islamic Revolution. The women contributed much more than before in the Revolution, and it was because the religious values were attracting a great number of women in the country. The superior leader of Iran wanted them all to be actively present in the social political grounds.

Women also participate in provincial activities such as public utility, social security, social selection, provincial and urban and rural election, economic activities, social activities, religious socialization, political involvement, ethnic or province ceremonies, and so on. When asked "what is the role of women in provincial activities?" Among the respondents, above 8 % said that women have a very high role in the provincial activities. And near (27.5%) of the respondents said that women have a high role in provincial activities. Moreover, around 50% of the respondents explained that the role of the women in the provincial activities is low, and lastly 14.5% of the respondent stated that the role of women in provincial activities is very low.

The next question put to the respondents was "Do you foresee any change in both quality and quantity of women's participation?" if 'yes' or 'no' then why? Majority (66.2%) of the respondents answered 'yes' they foresee lots of changes, such as:

(1) With women's participation, corruption will decline.

(2) With women's participation, people's belief in politics will increase.

(3) With women's participation, criminalization of politics will be reduced.

(4) Women will get rid of traditional authority of men.

(5) Increased participation will provide greater confidence in women and consequently women's problems will be solved.

And 33.8% of the respondents said no, they don't foresce any change because women's participation is less and also men do not allow the women to improve their social situation.

The above data shows the respondents level of political participation such as canvassing, agitations, political meeting, and hunger strikes. The majority of women had participated in voting regularly.

Furthermore, respondents believe that education, political experience, crime-free record, party manifesoc, cast/religion are important criteria in electing a candidate for political activities.

In addition, the study shows that most of the women, living in the research location, had participated in provincial activities such as public utility, social security, social election, province and urban and rural elections, economic activities, social activities, religious socialization, political involvement, ethnic or province ceremonies and so on.

Majority of the respondents predict lots of changes in both quality and quantity of politics if women participated in politics such as decline of corruption, increase of people's belief in politics, reduction of politics criminalization, and men's traditional authority towards women will be decreased, and increased participation will provide greater self-confidence in women, and as a result women's problems will be settled.

The frequency of political activities is cross tabulated against the level education, occupation, income and age of the respondents.

**Table 4.16: Age and Political Activities**

| *Political Activities* | *Age* | *Yes* | | *no* | | *sometime* | | *Total* |
|---|---|---|---|---|---|---|---|---|
| | | *Count* | *within age* | *Count* | *within age* | *Count* | *within age* | |
| Canvassing | 16-24 | 10 | 11.6 | 65 | 75.6 | 11 | 12.8 | 86 |
| | 25-34 | 12 | 17.6 | 48 | 70.6 | 8 | 11.8 | 68 |
| | 35-44 | 18 | 20.2 | 60 | 67.4 | 11 | 12.4 | 89 |
| | 45-54 | 3 | 6.0 | 39 | 78.0 | 8 | 16.0 | 50 |
| **Total** | | **43** | **14.7** | **212** | **72.4** | **38** | **13.0** | **293** |

| | | 1 | 2 | 3 | 4 | 5 | 6 | 7 |
|---|---|---|---|---|---|---|---|---|
| Agitations | 16-24 | 7 | 5.9 | 102 | 85.7 | 10 | 8.4 | 119 |
| | 25-34 | 5 | 6.3 | 67 | 83.8 | 8 | 10.0 | 80 |
| | 35-44 | 14 | 13.6 | 79 | 76.7 | 10 | 9.7 | 103 |
| | 45-54 | 3 | 5.1 | 52 | 88.1 | 4 | 6.8 | 59 |
| | 55above | 0 | .0 | 1 | 100.0 | 0 | .0 | 1 |
| **Total** | | **29** | **8.0** | **301** | **83.1** | **32** | **8.8** | **362** |
| Political meeting | 16-24 | 7 | 5.6 | 102 | 82.3 | 15 | 12.1 | 124 |
| | 25-34 | 2 | 2.6 | 69 | 90.8 | 5 | 6.6 | 76 |
| | 35-44 | 6 | 6.2 | 85 | 87.6 | 6 | 6.2 | 97 |
| | 45-54 | 2 | 3.6 | 51 | 91.1 | 3 | 5.4 | 56 |
| | 55above | 0 | .0 | 1 | 100.0 | 0 | .0 | 1 |
| **Total** | | **17** | **4.8** | **308** | **87.0** | **29** | **8.2** | **354** |
| Hunger-strikes | 16-24 | 73 | 56.2 | 39 | 30.0 | 18 | 13.8 | 130 |
| | 25-34 | 60 | 71.4 | 14 | 16.7 | 10 | 11.9 | 84 |
| | 35-44 | 64 | 61.5 | 30 | 28.8 | 10 | 9.6 | 104 |
| | 45-54 | 32 | 65.3 | 12 | 24.5 | 5 | 10.2 | 49 |
| | 55above | 0 | .0 | 1 | 100.0 | 0 | .0 | 1 |
| **Total** | | **229** | **62.2** | **96** | **26.1** | **43** | **11.7** | **368** |

**Table 4.17: Marital Situation and Political Activities**

| *Political Activities* | *Marital Situation* | *Yes* | | *No* | | *sometime* | | *Total* |
|---|---|---|---|---|---|---|---|---|
| | | *Count* | *%* | *Count* | *%* | *Count* | *%* | *Count* |
| | | 1 | 2 | 3 | 4 | 5 | 6 | 7 |
| Canvassing | Unmarried | 12 | 13.6 | 63 | 71.6 | 13 | 14.8 | 88 |
| | Married | 26 | 15.3 | 123 | 72.4 | 21 | 12.4 | 170 |
| | Divorce | 3 | 27.3 | 7 | 63.6 | 1 | 9.1 | 11 |
| | Widow | 3 | 23.1 | 9 | 69.2 | 1 | 7.7 | 13 |
| **Total** | | **44** | **15.6** | **202** | **71.6** | **36** | **12.8** | **282** |
| Agitations | Unmarried | 10 | 8.7 | 95 | 82.6 | 10 | 8.7 | 115 |
| | Married | 17 | 8.0 | 175 | 82.5 | 20 | 9.4 | 212 |
| | Divorce | 0 | .0 | 11 | 91.7 | 1 | 8.3 | 12 |
| | Widow | 1 | 8.3 | 11 | 91.7 | 0 | .0 | 12 |
| **Total** | | **28** | **8.0** | **292** | **83.2** | **31** | **8.8** | **351** |

| | | 1 | 2 | 3 | 4 | 5 | 6 | 7 |
|---|---|---|---|---|---|---|---|---|
| Political meeting | Unmarried | 8 | 6.9 | 96 | 82.8 | 12 | 10.3 | 116 |
| | Married | 6 | 3.0 | 180 | 90.0 | 14 | 7.0 | 200 |
| | Divorce | 2 | 15.4 | 10 | 76.9 | 1 | 7.7 | 13 |
| | Widow | 1 | 7.7 | 12 | 92.3 | 0 | .0 | 13 |
| **Total** | | **17** | **5.0** | **298** | **87.1** | **27** | **7.9** | **342** |
| Hunger-strikes | Unmarried | 73 | 59.8 | 32 | 26.2 | 17 | 13.9 | 122 |
| | Married | 137 | 63.1 | 56 | 25.8 | 24 | 11.1 | 217 |
| | Divorce | 4 | 40.0 | 5 | 50.0 | 1 | 10.0 | 10 |
| | Widow | 4 | 66.7 | 2 | 33.3 | 0 | .0 | 6 |
| **Total** | | **218** | **61.4** | **95** | **26.8** | **42** | **11.8** | **355** |

Table 4.18: Education and Political Activities

| *Political Activities* | *Educaton* | *Yes* | | *No* | | *sometime* | | *Total* |
|---|---|---|---|---|---|---|---|---|
| | | *Count* | *%* | *Count* | *%* | *Count* | *%* | *Count* |
| | | 1 | 2 | 3 | 4 | 5 | 6 | 7 |
| Canvassing | Illiterate | 0 | .0 | 10 | 90.9 | 1 | 9.1 | 11 |
| | Primary | 2 | 18.2 | 9 | 81.8 | 0 | .0 | 11 |
| | Secondary | 2 | 9.5 | 17 | 81.0 | 2 | 9.5 | 21 |
| | Diploma | 8 | 9.4 | 67 | 78.8 | 10 | 11.8 | 85 |
| | Graduation and above | 33 | 20.4 | 107 | 66.0 | 22 | 13.6 | 162 |
| **Total** | | **45** | **15.5** | **210** | **72.4** | **35** | **12.1** | **290** |
| Agitations | Illiterate | 0 | .0 | 12 | 92.3 | 1 | 7.7 | 13 |
| | Primary | 4 | 9.8 | 33 | 80.5 | 4 | 9.8 | 41 |
| | Secondary | 1 | 4.2 | 22 | 91.7 | 1 | 4.2 | 24 |
| | Diploma | 1 | 1.2 | 74 | 91.4 | 6 | 7.4 | 81 |
| | Graduation and above | 20 | 10.6 | 149 | 79.3 | 19 | 10.1 | 188 |
| **Total** | | **26** | **7.5** | **290** | **83.6** | **31** | **8.9** | **347** |

| | | 1 | 2 | 3 | 4 | 5 | 6 | 7 |
|---|---|---|---|---|---|---|---|---|
| Political meeting | Illiterate | 0 | .0 | 12 | 92.3 | 1 | 7.7 | 13 |
| | Primary | 0 | .0 | 38 | 95.0 | 2 | 5.0 | 40 |
| | Secondary | 0 | .0 | 21 | 95.5 | 1 | 4.5 | 22 |
| | Diploma | 6 | 7.1 | 73 | 85.9 | 6 | 7.1 | 85 |
| | Graduation and above | 10 | 5.6 | 156 | 87.2 | 13 | 7.3 | 179 |
| **Total** | | **16** | **4.7** | **300** | **88.5** | **23** | **6.8** | **339** |
| Hunger-strikes | Illiterate | 5 | 71.4 | 2 | 28.6 | 0 | .0 | 7 |
| | Primary | 9 | 23.1 | 27 | 69.2 | 3 | 7.7 | 39 |
| | Secondary | 16 | 64.0 | 7 | 28.0 | 2 | 8.0 | 25 |
| | Diploma | 74 | 75.5 | 11 | 11.2 | 13 | 13.3 | 98 |
| | Graduation and above | 122 | 65.9 | 39 | 21.1 | 24 | 13.0 | 185 |
| **Total** | | **226** | **63.8** | **86** | **24.3** | **42** | **11.9** | **354** |

**Table 4.19: Occupation and Political Activities**

| *Political Activities* | *Occupation* | *Yes* | | *No* | | *sometime* | | *Total* |
|---|---|---|---|---|---|---|---|---|
| | | *Count* | *%* | *Count* | *%* | *Count* | *%* | *Count* |
| 1 | 2 | 3 | 4 | 5 | 6 | 7 | 8 | 9 |
| Canvassing | Unemployed | 4 | 6.5 | 56 | 90.3 | 2 | 3.2 | 62 |
| | self employed, clerk, business women | 9 | 15.0 | 46 | 76.7 | 5 | 8.3 | 60 |
| | Students | 3 | 9.1 | 22 | 66.7 | 8 | 24.2 | 33 |
| | teacher, principle, govt. officer | 17 | 17.0 | 65 | 65.0 | 18 | 18.0 | 100 |
| | Doctor, engineer, lawyer, professor | 10 | 28.6 | 22 | 62.9 | 3 | 8.6 | 35 |
| **Total** | | **43** | **14.8** | **211** | **72.8** | **36** | **12.4** | **290** |

| 1 | 2 | 3 | 4 | 5 | 6 | 7 | 8 | 9 |
|---|---|---|---|---|---|---|---|---|
| Agitations | Unemployed | 0 | .0 | 73 | 97.3 | 2 | 2.7 | 75 |
| | self employed, clerk, business women | 6 | 7.6 | 66 | 83.5 | 7 | 8.9 | 79 |
| | Students | 1 | 3.3 | 26 | 86.7 | 3 | 10.0 | 30 |
| | teacher, principle, govt. officer | 13 | 12.5 | 81 | 77.9 | 10 | 9.6 | 104 |
| | Doctor, engineer, lawyer, professor | 7 | 10.1 | 54 | 78.3 | 8 | 11.6 | 69 |
| **Total** | | **27** | **7.6** | **300** | **84.0** | **30** | **8.4** | **357** |
| Political meeting | Unemployed | 0 | .0 | 74 | 98.7 | 1 | 1.3 | 75 |
| | self employed, clerk, business women | 6 | 7.8 | 63 | 81.8 | 8 | 10.4 | 77 |
| | Students | 1 | 3.0 | 27 | 81.8 | 5 | 15.2 | 33 |
| | teacher, principle, govt. officer | 5 | 5.2 | 85 | 87.6 | 7 | 7.2 | 97 |
| | Doctor, engineer, lawyer, professor | 4 | 6.1 | 56 | 84.8 | 6 | 9.1 | 66 |
| **Total** | | **16** | **4.6** | **305** | **87.6** | **27** | **7.8** | **348** |
| Hunger-strikes | Unemployed | 36 | 53.7 | 18 | 26.9 | 13 | 19.4 | 67 |
| | self employed, clerk, business women | 48 | 56.5 | 26 | 30.6 | 11 | 12.9 | 85 |
| | Students | 36 | 87.8 | 1 | 2.4 | 4 | 9.8 | 41 |
| | teacher, principle, govt. officer | 89 | 78.8 | 12 | 10.6 | 12 | 10.6 | 113 |
| | Doctor, engineer, lawyer, professor | 17 | 29.8 | 36 | 63.2 | 4 | 7.0 | 57 |
| **Total** | | **226** | **62.3** | **93** | **25.6** | **44** | **12.1** | **363** |

**Table 4.20: Income and Political Activities**

| *Political Activities* | *Income* | *Yes* | | *No* | | *Sometime* | | *Total* |
|---|---|---|---|---|---|---|---|---|
| | | *Count* | *%* | *Count* | *%* | *Count* | *%* | *Count* |
| 1 | 2 | 3 | 4 | 5 | 6 | 7 | 8 | 9 |
| Canvassing | No income | 11 | 11.5 | 76 | 79.2 | 9 | 9.4 | 96 |
| | Below1000 | 5 | 15.2 | 26 | 78.8 | 2 | 6.1 | 33 |
| | 1001-3000 | 11 | 13.3 | 59 | 71.1 | 13 | 15.7 | 83 |
| | 3001-6000 | 8 | 20.0 | 24 | 60.0 | 8 | 20.0 | 40 |
| | 6001 and above | 9 | 28.1 | 19 | 59.4 | 4 | 12.5 | 32 |
| **Total** | | **44** | **15.5** | **204** | **71.8** | **36** | **12.7** | **284** |
| Agitations | No income | 3 | 2.6 | 104 | 91.2 | 7 | 6.1 | 114 |
| | Below1000 | 3 | 7.5 | 35 | 87.5 | 2 | 5.0 | 40 |
| | 1001-3000 | 7 | 8.0 | 73 | 83.0 | 8 | 9.1 | 88 |
| | 3001-6000 | 5 | 11.1 | 35 | 77.8 | 5 | 11.1 | 45 |
| | 6001 and above | 10 | 14.5 | 50 | 72.5 | 9 | 13.0 | 69 |
| **Total** | | **28** | **7.9** | **297** | **83.4** | **31** | **8.7** | **356** |
| Political meeting | No income | 4 | 3.4 | 106 | 90.6 | 7 | 6.0 | 117 |
| | Below1000 | 1 | 2.7 | 32 | 86.5 | 4 | 10.8 | 37 |
| | 1001-3000 | 2 | 2.4 | 77 | 91.7 | 5 | 6.0 | 84 |
| | 3001-6000 | 3 | 7.1 | 34 | 81.0 | 5 | 11.9 | 42 |
| | 6001 and above | 6 | 9.0 | 54 | 80.6 | 7 | 10.4 | 67 |
| **Total** | | **16** | **4.6** | **303** | **87.3** | **28** | **8.1** | **347** |
| Hunger-strikes | No income | 78 | 64.5 | 26 | 21.5 | 17 | 14.0 | 121 |
| | Below1000 | 29 | 67.4 | 8 | 18.6 | 6 | 14.0 | 43 |
| | 1001-3000 | 72 | 75.0 | 14 | 14.6 | 10 | 10.4 | 96 |
| | 3001-6000 | 26 | 61.9 | 11 | 26.2 | 5 | 11.9 | 42 |
| | 6001 and above | 12 | 22.2 | 37 | 68.5 | 5 | 9.3 | 54 |
| **Total** | | **217** | **61.0** | **96** | **27.0** | **43** | **12.1** | **356** |

The result of cross-tabulations shows that attainment level are significant in the frequency of political activities, among respondents "the canvassing and agitation, political meeting and hunger strikes", have high attainment. Also we found out that in political activities, women with high education participated more. Furthermore the table reveals that women with "no income" and "income" both have attainments. Also, in "occupation" have higher attainment. Finally with "age" the younger age have more attainment.

The researcher has done a detailed study of some families to find out the political participation women in Tonekabon city.

1. Mrs Ahmadi, 37 years old, living in Khubanrazga, said that nowadays women are very active in political cases. For instance, they have the right to vote and be members of the parliament. Women take part in provincial activities such as public utility, social security, provincial urban and rural election, social activities, etc.

2. Mrs. Falah, 42 years old, living in the area of Azadi, is one of the active representatives of women in Tonekabon town. She says that women are very active in political participation such as canvassing, agitations, political meeting and hunger strikes. As representatives of women, they can solve women problems and make other women aware of their rights.

It is obvious from the case study of respondents that the women had political participation such as: canvassing, agitations, political meeting, hunger strikes and voting.

## Conclusion

Respondents' attitudes towards social life illustrated through their response. They said that women can be empowered by education, economic independence, bringing more women in politics, equal rights for both genders in all respects, by bringing a fundamental change in the prevailing mindset, by role fluidity, by having a strong voice in decision making process and by recognizing them as productive members of the society.

Regarding the sample group and 'visiting friends' and 'parties', majority of the respondents said they have been visiting friends regularly and sometimes they go to parties.

Most of the women under study agreed about giving equal rights of father/husband property to them and they believed that there is no difference between the genders in human rights; thus, 'equal right' is important especially for women.

Most respondents showed disdain for feminine stereotyping in cinema and advertising and supported their attitude by claiming that women's position is very high and they are not like goods.

Furthermore women believed that T.V. serials decrease women's position in family and society. Most of the time women are shown as powerless and weak members of the family and they should be just obedient of her husband and they haven't any role in family decision making.

In the present study, respondents were very positive of the value of education. They believed that education for both women and men are important and they must have equal opportunity for education. Moreover, they said both genders have the same ability and talent and there is no advantage in gender. In fact, women's education has direct influence on their life and increase family income, productivity, and social welfare.

Whereas the education is important for family, women's employment has positive role in family stability. And it is believed that education will change the people's approaches, values, and believes and also encourages them to family planning and birth-control. Majority of the respondents believed that there are strong links between a woman's education and her employment and income.

As the majority of respondents were in the married age group, typically some of them believed that women's employment had inherent risks of time management such as leisure for children's care and attention to the husband. Heavy work duty caused them to feel tired.

Regarding choosing a suitable occupation, among the respondents, more than half stated teaching is a respected occupation in society and a superior position. Also, there is more free time and more holidays comparing with other jobs. So they have more time to be at home and do their responsibility towards family. And some of the women were interested in other occupations such as; banking, being a physician or government officer, because of financial support, good income and social status.

In this study respondents stated that sometimes they suffer from disadvantages in the offices because of their gender. They added that for men is difficult to agree with women being in senior positions or boss. Besides; they imagine women are unable to do great work.

To establishing a balance between house and office they have regular time table to work at home and office. Sometimes their husband or parents help them to take care of children and home duty or they have servant at home.

They stated their work could help the family income and it improves family economic situation. Therefore they can provide more facility for family growth and progress.

In addition financial independence makes them powerful and influential, and they can share their income in family welfare. Whereas the economic situation is important for family, women employment have positive role in family stability.

This research shows women's employment influences in the family power structure. Education increases direct and indirect costs and economic benefits. Women's social status would lead to major changes in socio-economical variables in the country. Almost all the respondents state that job is important because, it keeps 'family stability' and helps 'family economy'.

Majority of the respondents believe that financial independence has a great impact. Because financial independence increases women's empowerment, women can participate in family decision making; even sometimes they are more powerful than their husbands. Furthermore, their income helps the family welfare and women feel calm. Because Iranian society and economics moderrised and resembles foreign economics, the average cost of living is very high; so, it is difficult for men to provide the family with all necessities.

Additionally, the power structure of patriarchy within families, women's greater awareness, their social participation, employment and education, will transform their status in the family and society.

Almost all women belonging to different occupations such as: business persons, clerks, teachers, physicians, engineers, lawyers, university teachers, government officers, university students were satisfied with their job and were totally happy and pleased.

In Iran, one of the significant social changes are the emergence of families with two income sources both husband and wife. The Iranian new two-income family faces certain pressures arising from both the traditional division of labour in the family and the members' new responsibilities. If the conflict is not properly managed, it has a negative impact on the social unity and function of the family as well as the emotional and social health of the members. More than half of the respondents contribute to the family income to afford a daily life.

Moreover; the researcher found out women were politically active in: canvassing, agitations, political meeting, and hunger strikes, also, majority of women had participated in voting regularly.

It is worth mentioning that the interview revealed that participation increased among the educated women. Other criteria were: political experience, crime-free record, party manifestx, and caste/religion.

In addition, study shows that most of the women, living in the research location, had participated in provincial activities such as public utility, social security, social election, province and urban and rural election, economic activities, social activities, religious socialization, political involvement, ethnic or province ceremonies, and so on.

Most respondents felt certain that qualitative and quantitative changes in politics would occur when women participated more in politics, such as: decline of corruption, increase of people's belief in politics, reduction of politics, criminalization, and men's traditional authority towards women will be decreased, and increased participation will provide greater self-confidence in women, and as a result women's problems will be settled.

# 5

# Attitude toward Vital Characteristics of Women, Religious Activities, Customs and Beliefs in the Ceremonies

The present chapter is divided into three sections. The first section is concentrated on respondents' attitude towards the vital characteristics of women. The second section focuses on women's role in the religious activities. In the third section their attitude towards various customs and beliefs in traditional socio-cultural and religious ceremonies is studied.

## I. ATTITUDE TOWARDS THE VITAL CHARACTERISTICS OF WOMEN

This section concentrates on attitude towards the vital characteristics of women in Tonekabon city:

Gender roles have long been a part of the nature debate: traditional theories of gender usually assume that one's gender identity, and hence one's gender role, is naturally given. For example, it is often claimed that women are naturally fit to look after children. The idea that differences in gender roles originate in differences in biology has found support in parts of the scientific community.

Nineteenth century anthropologists sometimes used descriptions of the imagined life of Palaeolithic hunter-gatherer societies for evolutionary explanations for gender differences. For example, those accounts maintain that the need to take care of offspring may have limited the females, freedom to hunt and assume positions of power.

Feminine characteristics are expressed primarily through female gender roles and expectations, which vary between societies and generations, and thus, are thought of as feminine change from culture to culture and generation to generation. In this sense, the role that women play or come to play in society is largely determined by society's expectation of how they are supposed to act and behave, and in turn, shapes their feminine characteristics.

H. L Moor, (1989) said, 'One of the most outstanding contributions of the anthropology of women has been its sustained analysis of gender symbols and sexual stereotypes. However, the main problem facing researchers in this area is how to explain both, the enormous observable variations in cultural understandings of what the categories of 'man' and 'woman' mean, and the fact that certain notions about gender appear in a wide range in different societies'.

Attitudes towards gender constitute one of the important socio-cultural characteristics of all communities. It is used as the criteria to distinguish communities as male/female-oriented, or traditional/modern.

Moore (1989:187) said "Gender stereotypes focus on traits, role behaviours, occupations, and physical characteristics which combine to form consistent clusters of women."

In the present study in order to understand respondents' ideas toward vital characteristics of women, the following different questions on good mother, good wife, religious virtue, wearing *hejab*, (wearing scarf, trousers, *manto*), voting, outdoor work, education, communication, family supporter, were asked.

Majority (90%) of the respondents said that all items in the characteristics of women such as "to be a good mother, to be a good wife, to following religion virtue, wearing *hejab*, voting, outdoor work, education, communication, family supporter" are 'very important' and only 10% said that above-mentioned items are 'not important'.

The next question asked was "How do you evaluate motherhood in women? Why?" Most of the respondents (98%) said women's role as mother is 'very important' because in family everyone's growth and success depends on women's support, and children are trained by mother, only 10% answered women's motherhood is 'not important'.

Table 5.1: Women Characteristics

| *Women Characteristics* | | *Frequency* | *%* | *Valid %* |
|---|---|---|---|---|
| | | 1 | 2 | 3 |
| **Good mother** | Very important | 293 | 61.7 | 67.5 |
| | Important | 67 | 14.1 | 15.4 |
| | Average | 66 | 13.9 | 15.2 |
| | Not important | 8 | 1.7 | 1.8 |
| | Total | 434 | 91.4 | 100.0 |
| Missing | System | 41 | 8.6 | |
| Total | | 475 | 100.0 | |
| **Good wife** | Very important | 353 | 74.3 | 81.1 |
| | Important | 63 | 13.3 | 14.5 |
| | Average | 18 | 3.8 | 4.1 |
| | Not important | 1 | 0.2 | 0.2 |
| | Total | 435 | 91.6 | 100.0 |
| Missing | System | 40 | 8.4 | |
| Total | | 475 | 100.0 | |
| **Religion virtue** | Very important | 279 | 58.7 | 65.5 |
| | Important | 96 | 20.2 | 22.5 |
| | Average | 35 | 7.4 | 8.2 |
| | Not important | 16 | 3.4 | 3.8 |
| | Total | 426 | 89.7 | 100.0 |
| Missing | System | 49 | 10.3 | |
| Total | | 475 | 100.0 | |
| **Hijab (wearing)** | Very important | 222 | 46.7 | 52.6 |
| | Important | 124 | 26.1 | 29.4 |

| | | 1 | 2 | 3 |
|---|---|---|---|---|
| | Average | 48 | 10.1 | 11.4 |
| | Not important | 28 | 5.9 | 6.6 |
| | Total | 422 | 88.8 | 100.0 |
| Missing | System | 53 | 11.2 | |
| Total | | 475 | 100.0 | |
| **vote depended** | Very important | 222 | 46.7 | 52.5 |
| | Important | 141 | 29.7 | 33.3 |
| | Average | 48 | 10.1 | 11.3 |
| | Not important | 12 | 2.5 | 2.8 |
| | Total | 423 | 89.1 | 100.0 |
| Missing | System | 52 | 10.9 | |
| Total | | 475 | 100.0 | |
| **Outdoor work** | Very important | 180 | 37.9 | 42.2 |
| | Important | 149 | 31.4 | 34.9 |
| | Average | 89 | 18.7 | 20.8 |
| | Not important | 9 | 1.9 | 2.1 |
| | Total | 427 | 89.9 | 100.0 |
| Missing | System | 48 | 10.1 | |
| Total | | 475 | 100.0 | |
| **Education** | Very important | 225 | 47.4 | 52.8 |
| | Important | 130 | 27.4 | 30.5 |
| | Average | 59 | 12.4 | 13.8 |
| | Not important | 12 | 2.5 | 2.8 |
| | Total | 426 | 89.7 | 100.0 |
| Missing | System | 49 | 10.3 | |
| Total | | 475 | 100.0 | |
| **Communication** | Very important | 194 | 40.8 | 52.7 |
| | Important | 110 | 23.2 | 29.9 |
| | Average | 60 | 12.6 | 16.3 |
| | Not important | 4 | 0.8 | 1.1 |
| | Total | 368 | 77.5 | 100.0 |

| | | 1 | 2 | 3 |
|---|---|---|---|---|
| Missing | System | 107 | 22.5 | |
| Total | | 475 | 100.0 | |
| **Family supporter** | Very important | 228 | 48.0 | 65.3 |
| | Important | 69 | 14.5 | 19.8 |
| | Average | 48 | 10.1 | 13.8 |
| | Not important | 4 | .8 | 1.1 |
| | Total | 349 | 73.5 | 100.0 |
| Missing | System | 126 | 26.5 | |
| Total | | 475 | 100.0 | |

It is also clear, from the Table, 5.1 that most of the respondents believed: all the characteristics of women are important.

It is clear from data that some of the respondents believed that some factors characterize traditional women, such as: good mother, good wife, family supporter. The characteristics of modern women not only are good mother, good wife, and family supporter which are characteristics of traditional women. But there are also additional characteristics such as: education, vote depended, outdoor worker, independent women depicts modern women. The virtue and wearing *hejab* are characteristics of religious women. The characteristics of a religious woman encompass the features of both modern and traditional women. We can see that all of women's characteristics are important in the community.

The researcher has done a detailed study of some families to find out the attitude towards the vital characteristics of women.

1. Mrs. Rahimi, 30 years old, living in Khuban Razga, is a teacher. Regarding women's attitudes she says that today's women can progress in different aspects by educating themselves, especially they can improve their awareness of bringing up the children. A good mother can be active both at home and outside home. So, by making a good plan and

sharing the responsibilities with the husband women can be active.

2. Mrs. Amini, 35 years old, living in the area of Goleijan, can bring joy to the family. These days' husbands and wives live with each other more peacefully and they do both the housework and their job. In the past women would do only the housework because it was their husband's wish. But today, women have changed and they prefer to follow a career.

3. Mrs. Emam, 27 years old, who is a student, says that she studies because she does not want to be only a house wife in future. By educating herself, she wants to be financially independent in future.

4. Mrs. Ahmadi, 37 years old, living in Arian area, says that women must plan to work and also do the house work with the help of their husbands. She says "why only wives should do the housework? Husbands can be very helpful in doing the housework.

It is clear from the case study that the respondents believed that, in addition to the traditional characteristics of good woman, such as: good mother, good wife, family supporter, the following characteristics such as religion virtue, outdoor work, education, communication, family supporter, financial independence, independent women are also very important characteristics for women.

## II. THE ROLE OF THE WOMEN IN RELIGIOUS ACTIVITIES

This section is devoted to role of women in religious activities in Tonekabon city.

The word 'religion' has been derived from the root word 'religio', which means "to bind together", and religion actually does it. Intro, Elmers Miller,Charles A. Weitz, (1979:548) said "Religion is the system of social interactions consisting of those beliefs and activities that order human life by relating humans to spiritual beings and powers." Religion is a way of responding to a longing in the human spirit for a richer, fuller life, for liberation, by mitigating the negativities of life, such as, anxieties and guilt, on the one side and on other by promoting and strengthening positive experience on the other.

Religion is one of the most ancient, universal and enduring components of human existence. It is also a vital force that affects both the individuals and the society. It is the core of any culture, influencing any thoughts, attitudes, emotions, values and socio-political and economic structures. It is a complete and all-embracing, all encompassing system of meaning and relations based on which many aspects of social relations are explained and handled which otherwise would have been difficult. It is a meaning-giving system of human society. It reinforces faith and hope in life, enables persons to cope with and reorients it. It legitimizes many things and links human beings to the supernatural and provides integrity to the society and psychic unity to its members.

Religion is a system of symbols which acts to establish powerful, pervasive, and long lasting moods and motivations in men by formulating conception with such an aura of factuality that the moods and motivations are seen uniquely realistic. Geertz (1975:90) as explicated by many scholars, said "religion is a cultural universal". All the other institutions are integrated and operate around it .Religion is a part of culture. It has its own purpose, which served the humanity. When the people of particular religion are not satisfied with the established religion, they tend to change their religion. If the religion or culture is not adaptive to the needs of the particular society, people go for alternatives, which cater to their needs.

"Islam" is the name of a religion, and it comes from the Arabic root word meaning "peace" and "submission." and a person who believes in and follows Islam is called a "Muslim." Also, Muslim believes in God and prays to Him. Moreover, they believe that prayer is one of the greatest forms of worship that God likes his servants to offer. In Iran, majority of people are Muslim, so that religion, in general and Islam in particular have important role in the society. Muslims in Iran are divided into two parts; 'Shias' and 'Sunnis'. And majority of Muslims in Iran are 'Shias'.

Carroll Foster, Theodora (1983:253) said, 'religion everywhere is in a state of flux, pushed and pulled by conservative and liberal forces. Whichever wins, traditionalism or reform, will have major repercussions for development and women. Women ultimately will have to decide for themselves whether they want to be part of the development and modernization. If they do, they will need to resist being buffeted and manipulated by male-dominated religious forces. For most, this will be difficult. They will need help and encouragement to develop an understanding that they can continue to be faithful adherents to their religions and yet expect to be treated as full, intelligent human beings.'

Each religion has an innate flexibility and considerable scope for helping women to reach their potential. But will religious leaders be prepared to yield that option to women? Will they continue to resist women's full integration into development in all its multifaceted aspects: spiritual, educational, economic, social, and political? Will they be aided and abetted by the laity, politicians, development planners, and others, ignoring women's presence and needs resisting their full incorporation into development?

Since the majority of the population in Iran are Moslem and near half of the population are women, so women's religious activity is more important. Women participate in both public and private religious ceremonies. Public religious ceremonies include those programs which are performed in streets, mosques, and other public places. Private religious ceremonies include those programs that are at home or some private places where men are not allowed to participate. In order to find out the role of women in religious activities, question put to the respondents was: "What is the role of women in religious activities?" To this question most of the respondents (78.6%) stated that women have very important role in religious activities. Because women believed in religion more than men. And around 21.6% of the respondents feel that women's role in religious activities is low, because they do not believe in such activities.

Moslem people believe in God, resurrection, soul, hell, heaven, and ghost and since the majority of the population in Iran are Moslem, so the researcher wanted to find out how much they believed in religious ceremonies.

The next question was "what is your idea about, belief in God, resurrection, soul, hell, heaven, and ghost". And if 'no' why? To a question, on their opinion about believing in God all (100%) respondents answered positively. God influences the individual's social and private life and it lead to the acceptance of religious believes and is followed by the improvement in moral and religious values. Nearly 98.6% of the respondents said they believe in resurrection because they believe that man will have rebirth after death by resurrection and they will respond to their behaviour (any positive or negative action by man) in this world and only (1.4%) said they didn't believe in resurrection. And above 96.6% answered they believe in hell and heaven, because some people believe that they will go to heaven or hell after death and it depends on their behaviour (any positive or negative action by man) in this world. And a few (3.1%) answered they didn't believe in hell and heaven. Meanwhile around (58.5%) of the respondents stated that they believe in ghost. According to religion, man has two dimensions: first, is body and the second is soul, and after death his body will be ruined, and his soul will remain and by resurrection again the body and soul will join and will be present in resurrection. And nearly 41.5% respondents said they don't believe in ghosts. And when researcher asked them "why they don't believe in resurrection, soul, hell, heaven, and ghost" they answered because they deny the existence of resurrection, soul, hell, heaven, and ghost.

Saying prayers is of great importance among Muslims, and it is considered as the basic foundation of Islam.

The next question put to the respondents was "How many times do you pray to God?" Around 66% of the respondents said they pray to God according to religious role every day. "Namaz" is the name for the necessary prayers which are performed five times a day, and are a direct link between the worshipper and God with no earthly intermediaries. A prayer takes a few minutes to perform. Prayer, obligatory and spontaneous, is an enormous spiritual treasure to be valued. It encourages peace, purity and tranquillity and instills companionship with God. And nearly 25% of respondents answered that, they do some times pray to God. Only 1% of the respondents said that they never pray to God. But they believed in God and only don't pray.

The other question was "do you get calm with religion?" if 'yes' or 'no' why? Almost 97% of the respondents said 'yes' because "we are Moslem and according to holy book (Quran), man can talk to God and this direct link will give them calmness and tranquillity". Religion offers its followers tranquillity and makes their life meaningful. And only 3% said they will not be calm by religion. Because they do not believe in religion, therefore it doesn't give them tranquillity and calm.

Since statistics show that the majority of Iranian citizens are Muslim, in Tonekabon city most of the women have been doing religious activities in public and private religious ceremonies include those programs that are performed at home or some private places where men are not allowed to enter; and elder women are more active in religious programs.

Since most of the people under study believed in God, they believed God influences the individual's social and private life and it leads to the acceptance of religious believes and is followed by the improvement in moral and religious values. Most of the women in the study believed in God, resurrection, soul, hell, heaven and ghost.

Saying prayers is of great importance among Muslims, and it is considered as the basic foundation of Islam. The present study shows that most of the respondents pray to God by "Namaz". "Namaz" is the name for the compulsory prayers which are performed five times a day, and it is a direct link between the worshipper and God with no earthly intermediaries. A prayer takes a few minutes to be performed.

Prayer, obligatory and spontaneous, is an enormous spiritual treasure to be valued. It encourages peace, purity and tranquillity and instils companionship with God. There is no change in the lifestyle as long as religious activities are concerned.

In a social research regarding cultural changes in Iran, Azad Armaky and Gheyasvand (2003) believe that "God" has a major role in an individual's life and deeds, the way it makes them accept the religion and go for practices concerned. Based on the research, more than 90% of the questioned people believed that religion gives them a sort of relief and capability.

Amir Neekpay, (2001), in his study "Reviewing changes regarding religion in contemporary Iran", says that there is a close relationship between religious belief and practicing a religion. According to the researcher, social religious practices are not so frequent among youth in Iran, not so many of them go to the mosques or participate in charity acts. It is often told that women are more traditional and more religious compared with men.

The researcher has done a detailed study of some families to find out the respondents participation in religious activities.

1. Mrs. Mehrabi, 35 years old and living in Goleijan area, is a member of the religious association of the city. Regarding religious participation she says the activities of women in religion maybe more than men. She also believed that women are very active in holding religious ceremonies such as celebrating the birthdays of different Imams. Also people mourn on the dates which the Imams passed away. Women

are more interested in travelling to religious cities such as Mashhad, Ghom or Mecca in Saudi Arabia.

2. Mrs. Hoseini, 50 years old, is a housewife. She said that religious beliefs are part of us and our lives. Women are loyal to religion; they follow their religion and they participate in all religious ceremonies such as Moharam and Safar. During the month of Moharam, one of the Imams (Imam Hosein) was martyred. Mrs Hoseini, every year during Moharam, cooks food and gives it to people. Her daughter says that it is better to give the money to the poor instead. However, the ways of thinking of the new generation are different from the old generation.

It is clear from the case study that, women participation in religious activities maybe more. They participate in all religious ceremonies such as Moharam and Safar. During the month of Moharam, one of the Imams (Imam Hussein) was martyred. And women are very active in holding religious ceremonies such as celebrating the birthdays of Imams.

## III. ATTITUDE TOWARD VARIOUS CUSTOMS AND BELIEFS IN TRADITIONAL SOCIO- CULTURAL AND RELIGIOUS CEREMONIES

This section concentrates on attitude toward various customs and beliefs in traditional, socio-cultural and religious ceremonies of women in Tonekabon city:

The range of studies of socio-cultural, religious ceremony and marriage is wide and concerns itself with human culture and societies. It studies social behaviour, generally in institutionalized forms. One of the most important functions of religious ceremony is to give meaning to and explain those aspects of physical and social environment that are not fully understood through normal experience and thought.

There are many ceremonies in Iran. One of the most important of them is Nooroz. "Norooz" was started by a mythical Persian emperor, Shah Jamshid, from Achaemenid Dynasty (500 BC). Achaemenid created the first major empire in the region and built Persepolis complex (Takhte Jamshid) in the city of Shiraz. Norooz in Persian means "New Day" that is the first day of spring. It brings hope, peace and prosperity to the world and has been celebrated among people regardless of ethnic background, political views or religion in many countries around the globe such as Iran, Afghanistan, Azerbaijan, Turkey, Uzbekistan, Pakistan, Georgia, Iraq, Tajikistan, Syria, Armenia and India. Some of the activities during Norooz are cleaning, buying new clothes, and painting eggs, family reunion, giving presents, visiting neighbours and friends and celebrating by having a picnic on the 13th day of spring.

Celebration, of Norooz, always begins on the first day of spring. Norooz ceremonies are symbolic representations of two ancient concepts - the end and the rebirth; or good and evil. A few weeks before the New Year, Iranians clean and rearrange their homes. They make new clothes, bake pastries and germinate seeds as sign of renewal. There is also a spread in which there are seven items, each symbolizes a wish. All seven items in this ceremonial table start with the Persian letter "Seen" or S in English. The "Haft Seen" spread is usually put out a week before the New Year, which sets the mood for celebration. The seven items are "Sabzeh" (grown wheat or lentil) for rebirth, "Samanu" (flour and sugar) for sweetness of life, "Sekeh" (coin ) for prosperity and wealth, "Senjed" (dried fruit of Lotus tree) for love, "Seer" (garlic) for health, "Somaq" ( sumac berries) for warmth and "Serkeh" (vinegar) for patience. Also, there are other items on the Norooz spread such as painted eggs, which represent fertility, a mirror that represents image and reflection of life, and a goldfish in a bowl that represents life.

In the present study the respondents were asked the following questions: "How much do you believe in Norooz (New Year)?" Why? Nearly 97.5% of the respondents said Norooz ceremony is 'important' because that is an old tradition. Also, Norooz is a symbol of ancient Persia and brings hope, friendship, peace, tranquillity, success and prosperity to the world especially in Persia. And only 2.5% of the respondents' stated Norooz ceremony is less important because 'we live in a modern world and Norooz dates back to the past.

Religious ceremonies are also of great importance in Iran. In such ceremonies, people go to religious places in cities of Iran such as Mashhad and Ghom. Pilgrims go to Saudi Arabia, the city of Mecca, to perform the religious ceremony of Omreh. Usually, pilgrims stay in Saudi Arabia for two weeks. They spend seven days in Medina and the next seven days in Mecca. The religious ceremony of Omreh is performed in Mecca. Pilgrims stay in Medina because the great Nabi Mosque is located there; they visit the mosque to pray and to purify themselves.

Mashhad is one of the most important religious cities in Iran because Imam Reza is buried there. Muslims believe in twelve Imams and Imam Reza is the eighth Imam.

Ghom is another important religious city of Iran where Hazrate Masoumeh is buried. Hazrate Masoumeh is the sister of Imam Reza. A lot of people go to Mecca, Mashhad, Ghom and other religious cities in order to seek remedies for illnesses or diseases because they believe that if they pray in such places, their prayers will be answered. Also people of Iran travel to other religious countries such as Arabia and Syria. Religious journeys have great importance among the people of Iran.

And the other question was "How much do you believe in pilgrimage? "Why? Above 85.8% of the respondents said they believed in (visit to) pilgrimage, because they are Muslim and they follow all Islamic ceremonies. And only 14.2% said they don't believe in (visit to) pilgrimages.

In the present study majority of respondents stated that Norooz ceremony is very important. They believed that Norooz is a symbol of ancient Persia and brings peace, tranquillity, success and prosperity.

The majority of people in Iran are Muslim pilgrim's. They visit some pilgrinage in Iran and abroad.

The researcher has done a detailed study of some families to find out the attitude toward social culture and religious ceremony of women in Tonekabon city.

1. Mrs. Mirzai, 35 years old, living in Tonekabon Mahal, said that Norooz is our traditional ceremony and we must cling to it and not let it change. Norooz is not only the beginning of the New Year; it is also the cause of purity in us. She says that during Norooz, we visit the old relatives and friends. So, Norooz is the time of visiting each other.

2. Mrs. Abasi, 52 years old, living in Arian area, says that Norooz reminds us of the past. We remember wearing new clothes and other things.

3. Mrs. Rahmati, 50 years old, living in Karim Abad, says that every country has its own rituals and they must be respected. We have not forgotten Norooz and we must never forget it; especially, the new generation should remember it always.

It is obvious from the case study that Norooz ceremony is a traditional ceremony and it should be celebrated religiously and not allowed to change.

## Marriage Ceremony

Marriage in Iran cannot be dissolve accept in a very exceptional case. The importance of marriage transcendent not only the entire family but also the ancestral lineage as the well as future generation.

K.N. Dash, (2004:46) stated that, "Marriage is a social institution machinery by which society enables people to satisfy their biological needs in an orderly way. It is relatively more universal and major social institution because it fulfils one of the most important functions of the society and reproduction with some degree of social regulation over sex relationship. In contemporary world it is impossible to find any society in which marriage, in any form could be entirely absent."

Marriage and family are complementary concepts. Marriage is an institution and family is the association that embodies the institution. Marriage has existed in every form of society from time immemorial. Based on Iranian scriptures, marriage system in Iran was well established in Zoroastrian Period. From ancient times, marriage is considered as a ritual and sacramental union.

For Iranians, marriage is an event, which must be celebrated not quietly but with glory and distinction. It is the most conspicuous of all the occasions and is celebrated in the presence of a fairly large assembly. In the past, the parents and older members of the family arranged almost all marriages. This is still the case in rural areas and with traditional families. Modern couples however, choose their own mate but their parents' consent is still very important and is considered by both sides. Even with modern Iranians, after the couple have decided themselves, it is normally the grooms' parents or other relatives who take the initiative and formally ask for the bride and her family's consent. Once this is done then the marriage will be announced. Marriage customs are different in different cities of Iran. However, today, people of Iran do not cleave to the customs of the past; sometimes people do not follow the traditional marriage customs.

In the ancient times, the musicians playing at marriage gatherings used drums to announce the marriage to the people of the town or village. The group that gathered for the marriage was called the assembly for the queenly bride. Traditionally, both the bride and the bridegroom dressed in white with garlands of flower on their necks. The white colour is a symbol of purity, innocence and faithfulness. Traditionally, boys and girls were never to see each-other until the wedding. But today in Iran, boys and girls like romantic love. Boy and girls fall in love and then make the decision on their own to get married. However, the dynamic forces of urbanization, industrialization and increased education have introduced new elements into the marriage.

In order to find out role of women in marriage, the question put to the respondents was "How do you evaluate women's marriage?" Why? Nearly 96.9% of the respondents said that women's marriage is 'important' because woman can live married life and she can be a good mother and a good wife; furthermore, marriage is a very important custom according to Islam, and life cycle will be continued', and 3.1% of the respondents said that women's marriage is 'not important' because 'women can live alone without husband.

The marriage ceremony marks the most significant ritual for all Iranians specially the women.

And the other question was how do you feel the 'Khastegari' (proposing marriage) that is "wooing customs" in recent decade?" Why? Nearly (85.5%) of the respondents said the wooing custom is 'important' because in "wooing" two member of the family will be more familiar with each other and in fact it is the way to fasten the family friendship. Moreover, wooing is an old custom which passes from generation to generation. "Wooing" is held before the wedding party in which the families of the bride and the groom meet and negotiate or talk about the date of the wedding, payment, price custom, marriage contract, engagement, etc. In "wooing" usually the elders of the families such as parents and the grandparents are present. Also, nearly 14.5% stated wooing custom is 'not important' because they don't believe in wooing custom' and say it is just a formality and it is not necessary.

The next question put to the respondents was "How do you feel about the 'Namzadi' that is engagement customs" in recent decades? Nearly 90% of the respondents answered the engagement custom is important because it is a kind of marriage celebration and gives pleasure and memorable time for both couples and their families. The "engagement custom" is held after the "wooing custom" in which the groom's family gives gifts like a ring, clothes and cookies or sweets to the bride. In "engagement custom" the close relatives of both sides of the two families are invited. And, only 10% of the respondents explained that the engagement custom is not important because in engagement ceremony couples or their families have to spend lots of money. They added instead of engagement ceremony, couples could buy some items for the new home.

And the next question was "what do you feel about 'Aghd' "marriage contract" customs in recent decades?" Mostly (97%) of the respondents stated the marriage contract customs are 'important' because in fact it is an official contract between man and woman as a couple and according to Islam marriage contract should be written officially. Also, they believed that marriage contract develops; and increases stability of common life. The "marriage and marriage contract custom" is held after "the engagement custom" in which both the bride and the groom go to a hair dressing saloon and wear formal clothes. The bride's formal clothes have always been a white dress and the groom's clothes have always been a suit. Then the bride's parents' home is made ready for the celebration with a special decoration, sofre, Quran, sugar-candy (*nabat*), fruits, cookies, flowers, etc. Then a Molla must come to marry the bride and the groom. The Molla (clergy man) reads a sura (khotbeye aghd). Then the groom's family gives gifts to the bride. In this day and age the bride's family also gives gifts to the groom's family. And very less (3%) said that the marriage and marriage contract custom is 'not important'.

And the other question was 'how do you think about the 'Mahrieh' that is "marriage payments customs" in recent decades? Why? Majority (91.1%) said it is important because "Mahrieh" (marriage payments) is a gift from the groom for the bride and it is given in the form of money or gold coins. The amount of this money is agreed by the families of the bride and the groom, is a source of financial security for married women in case of divorce or widowhood. The criterion for deciding the number of coins is the year in which the bride was born. For example if the bride was born in 1980, the number of coins will be 1980. Of course today a lot of people use the year in which the bride was born to come to agreement about the number of the gold coins. The groom must pay the payment when the bride demands. Nearly 8.9% of the respondents replied that it is not important because sometimes marriage payments make problem for the couples and it is not any safety for their life.

The other question was "How do you feel about the 'Sheer Bahaa' that is bride price customs in recent decades?" Why? Nearly 54% answered the "Sheer Bahaa" (bride price) is important 'because it is custom and agreement upon money or gift given. "Bride price" is a gift to the bride's mother for having nursed her to the bride's family. Now part of the marriage portion is settled beforehand in cash. And also 46% of the respondents stated that the bride price customs is 'not important' because it depends upon the person' and bride's family.

Most of the respondents under study believed that women's marriage is important according to Islam and for continuing of life cycle. Women can have married life and they can be a good mother and good wife. The marriage ceremony marks the most significant ritual for all Iranians specially the women such as; Khastegari, Namzadi, Aghd, Mahrieh, Sheer Bahaa.

## Conclusion

The majority of respondents expressed their ideas about some factors which characterize traditional women, such as: good mother, good wife, family supporter. The characteristics of modern women are not only good mother, good wife, and family supporter, which are also characteristics of traditional women. But there are also additional characteristics such as: education, vote depended, outdoor worker, independent women, which depict modern women. The virtue and wearing *hejab* are characteristics of religious women. The characteristics of a religious woman encompass the features of both modern and traditional women. We can see that all of women's characteristics are important in the community.

Women's religious participation is more important, as the majority of the population in Iran are Muslim and nearly half the population are women. Most of the women living in Tonekabon city, had participated in both public and private religious ceremonies. Public religious ceremonies include those programs which are performed in streets, mosques, and other public places. Private religious ceremonies include those programs that are performed at home or some private places where men are not allowed to enter. Of course elder women are more activite in religious programs.

Majority of the respondents believe in God. And God influences the individual's social and private life and leads to the acceptance of religious believes and is followed by the improvement in moral and religious values. Majority of the women in this study believe in God, resurrection, soul, hell, heaven, and ghost.

According to the present study, most of the respondents pray to the God by "Namaz". "Namaz" is the name for the compulsory prayers performed five times a day, and it is considered to be a direct link between the worshipper and the God with no earthly intermediaries. A prayer takes a few minutes to be performed.

Prayer, obligatory and spontaneous, is an enormous spiritual treasure to be valued. It encourages peace, purity and tranquillity and instils companionship with God.

In this study, respondents believed on Norooz (New Year) ceremony which is very important, because it is an old tradition. And Norooz is a symbol of ancient Persia and brings hope, friendship, peace, tranquillity, success and prosperity to the world especially in Persia. The first day of spring is the beginning of Norooz. Before spring Iranian people prepare themselves for Norooz by cleaning their homes. Most of the wedding parties in Iran are held during the Norooz holiday which is two weeks.

As all respondents are Muslim women, they believed in all Islamic ceremonies including pilgrimage; and they go to important religious cities in Iran, such as Mashhad and Ghom to pray. Some people believe that if they visit pilgrim places and ask God to cure some diseases, their prayer will be fulfilled; in other words, God will answer their prayers. In addition to this there are two important cities such as Mecca and Medina in Saudi Arabia. Every year lots of pilgrims go there to perform the religious ceremony.

Most respondents studied herein believed that marriage was useful for women because a woman can benefit from married life and she can be a good mother and a good wife; furthermore, marriage is important according to Islam and life cycle will be continued. Marriage and family are complementary concepts. Marriage is an institution and family is the association that embodies the institution. Marriage has existed in every form of society from time immemorial. Based on Iranian scriptures, marriage system in Iran was well established in Zoroastrian Period. From ancient times, marriage is considered as a ritual and sacramental union.

Among the many traditional customs in Iran, most respondents here believed in 'Khastegari' that is "wooing custom". According to them that is important custom' because wooing is a traditional custom. Through this 'Wooing custom' two member of the family will become more familiar with each other and it is the way to fasten the family friendship.

Also about the "Namzadi", that is 'engagement customs', respondents said, this is important because it is a kind of marriage celebration and gives pleasure and memorable time for both couples and families. . The "engagement custom" is held after the "wooing custom" in which the groom's family gives gifts like a ring, clothes and cookies or sweets to the bride. In "engagement custom" the close relatives of both sides of the two families are invited.

The respondents felt that the marriage contract or 'Aghd', was important, because it is an official contract between man and woman as a couple. In addition according to Islam marriage contract should be written officially. Also, they believed that marriage contract develops and increases stability of common life.

Majority believed that Mahrieh, that is "marriage payments" custom is important because "Mahrieh" is a gift from the groom for the bride and it is given in the form of money or gold coins. The amount of this money is a source of financial security for married women in case of divorce or widowhood. In a rapidly-changing, modern society, women need not depend entirely upon their husband or children.

Most of the respondents believed on Sheer Bahaa (bride price custom). They said that it is important because it is a tradition of agreement upon money or gift given to the bride's family. "Bride price" is a gift to the bride's mother for having nursed her. Now part of the marriage portion settled upon the wife which is paid beforehand in cash.

The women, under study, attached great importance to education and income and have shown a strong, positive, attitude towards education and income. They consider education and income as a key to change and one of the important forces in building their status.

It is clear in this chapter that respondents have strong positive attitude toward vital characteristics of women such as "good mother, good wife, religious virtue, wearing hejab, voting, outdoor work, education, communication, and family supporter". In addition to this they also had positive attitude toward ceremony such as Norooz (New Year) and visit to pilgrimages and marriage customs such as Khastegari. Namzadi, Aghd, Mahrieh and Sher Bahaa.

Therefore we can say that there is not much change in the lifestyle in nonmaterial culture such as religious activities, religious ceremonies traditional ceremonies and some traditional customs and believes of marriage ceremonies.

# 6
# Conclusion

In this concluding chapter the researcher has reviewed some of the main points made in the previous chapters, with particular emphasis on change in the lifestyle of the women, with reference to the women of Tonekabon city. Leisure time activity is one of the most important factors of studying the change in lifestyle.

The researcher has focused on Kaplan's Six categories of leisure activity, namely sociability, association, game, art, movement and immobility. In the present study, the respondents stated that most of the women spend their leisure time according to traditional pattern such as: visiting the park, public library, museum, historical places, celebrating festivals, and doing social work. And as regarding modern pattern of spending leisure time such as; gym, body building clubs, cinema, museum, concert hall, exhibition, tourist place, voyage hobbies, restaurant, fast food restaurant, coffee shops and social work. Many young respondents clearly spent lots of time in modern pattern of leisure time activities. So we can observe both traditional and modern pattern of spending leisure time. So we can say that to some extent there is change in the lifestyle as for as leisure time activities are concerned and there is also continuity in some respect.

Also in the case study, respondents spend their leisure time in traditional pattern such as: going to parks, doing social work, going out or to a neighbour, going to religious cities, watching TV and listening to radio, visiting mother's family and some times with in-law's family. And also spend leisure

...ines

...ost of the respondents ..., they also participate in other ...ing, knitting, religious activities, studying, ... and embroidery work.

Moreover we can observe that, in the data of recreation pattern, women had participation in both modern and traditional level. In modern pattern including; reading newspapers and magazines, listening to radio, chess, sewing, knitting, embroidery works, studying, visiting attending parties, visiting clubs and the traditional pattern including, visiting neighbours, recreation with children, attending religious activities and resting.

Majority of the respondents under study like to make and decorate food and eat it at regular or fixed times. Some of the respondents go to restaurants at least once a month. The respondents stated that they use protein, vitamins, and calcium in their daily meals through the use of rice, oil, milk, vegetables, meat, eggs, and fish. It seems that most of the respondents have an awareness of the importance of eating nutritious food and balanced diet.

The present research shows that personal habits are of great importance, especially regarding food and nutrition. Also they believed that daily food must include the needed vitamins and proteins for children. They said that, they were cooking special food like fish and meat during the holidays.

Beside that, the majority of the respondents paid special attention to personal hygiene by bathing regularly, applying cosmetics and cutting or styling hair. Most of the respondents said that they visited beauty parlour each month. In addition to this, the present study shows that most of the women, living in the research location, used a means of body management, like nasal plastic surgery and heavy make-up especially among the young ladies either at home or in society. Nowadays, with regards to progress of technology and science, the lifestyle of women in body management has greaths changed.

In the present study, both traditional and modern houses have been viewed. In modern houses, everything such as furniture, carpet, colour, and decoration are set and are the latest mode. But in traditional houses everything is simple and old and related to traditions. Thus, one can observe and mark the contrasts between styles clearly.

Moreover, the case study shows that women's attitude toward lifestyle in the house has changed. In modern house, there is harmony among the colours and decoration in every thing such as furniture, carpet which are set and are selected from the latest modes.

Most of the women under study feel that sleeping is necessary for each and every person; and it depends on the nature of their jobs. So some of them have to get up early in the morning and like to sleep in silence. And few of the respondents said they have fixed sleeping time. In the case study, the relationship between working time and sleep is both critical and noticeable.

Over all, the attitude of the respondents toward work influences leisure in many ways. The majority of respondents under study stated that work time is regular. They believed work for women is very important, especially out of home; however, women have free time inside the home. Regarding the comparison between women and men in work, nearly half of the respondents believed that women and men have equal ability. This reflects a modern or post-modern feminist view of gender.

Traditional Iranian clothing has its roots extending back at least as far as thousands of years ago. Today, neither young girls residing in the provincial towns, nor the ones living in rural areas are any more interested in putting on their traditional garments.

Most of the new generations feel that western clothes are impressive, and convenient for every day wear, for formal and family occasions and functions in contrast with traditional garments. The important criteria for buying clothes to most respondents were fashion, beauty, quality, comfort and uniqueness. Also nearly half of the respondents said that they liked western and modern clothes because of their variety, better colour and better design, but half of them liked traditional clothes which includes scarf, shirt, *shalith* (a short creased skirt), vest, skirt, pants and shawl wrapped around their waist.

In addition, the present group interview shows that most participants reported that, they found fashion, quality, comfort and uniqueness as important for buying clothes. And in younger women under study they like more western clothes and wear moderns clothes. And of course different socio-economic conditions and income have an important role.

Concerning smoking, the majority of women under study said that they did not smoke. And few of them said that they smoke for relaxation, recreation, to have fun, they feel it is a mode of modern lifestyle. One important item is that, in Iran especially, in research study both modernised women and those with some modes in both old and new generation didn't like to smoke.

More recently Korzenny, Ting and Toomey (1992), have stated that one should distinguish between technological instruments and their actual use. Above all, one should avoid handing the uncertain social effectiveness of technology and mass media over to unscrupulous individuals who would use them for their own advantage. To avoid the domination of these tools, we must understand the interrelation between media, culture, ideology, state and individuals fully.

In addition, nowadays, mass media are the products of highly developed technologically oriented states. There is a strong impact of urbanization and modernisation on the women under study. As a result, in location of study, the information obtained from the respondents about their exposure to various media of mass communication like films, radio, newspapers, magazines, journals, T.V. and internet has been considerable. Data also indicated that majority of respondents listen to radio, and nearly 97% watch T.V./movie. The majority of respondents read newspapers and magazines, and read particularly information such as international news, political, women news, culture, art and sport news, stories, poems, articles, social news, economics and current topic.

As regards their exposure to internet, more than half of women under study were familiar with new technology such as internet. And new generation used internet more in leisure time, specially for chatting.

Amit Kumar Gupta (1986) reported that many experts on the topic regarded economic setting as the "social field" and determines the status and roles of women of the times. Among dominant influences within are the family structure, usually a patriarchal system, and related domestic phases, affected by the setting and which respond by affecting the societal attitude towards women. Thus, the interrelations between these three factors-economic setting, family structure and women's status-exposes a number of important considerations.

In the present study, the respondents have strong attitudes towards social life. They said that women can be empowered by education, economic independence, bringing more women into politics, equal rights for both sexes in all respects, by bringing a fundamental change in the prevailing mindset, by role fluidity, by having a strong voice in decision-making process and by recognizing them as productive members of the society.

On finding about women 'visiting friends' and 'parties', majority of the respondents said they have been visiting friends regularly and sometimes they go to parties.

Most of the women under study agreed about giving equal rights of father/husband's property to them and they believed that there is no difference between the sexes in human rights; thus, 'equal right' is important especially for women.

Majority of the respondents believed that women should reject being portrayed as commodities in cinema/ advertisements. They said women's position is very high and they are not like goods.

Furthermore women believed that T.V. serials decrease women's position in family and society. Most of the time women are shown as powerless and weak members of the family and they should be just obedient to their husbands and they haven't any role in family decision-making.

In the present study, respondents stated positive approach to education. They believed that education for both women and men are important and they must have equal opportunity for education. Moreover, they said both sexes have the same ability and talent and there is no advantage in gender. In fact, women's education has direct influence on their life and increases family income, productivity, and social welfare.

Whereas the education is important for family, women's employment has positive role in family stability. And it is believed that education will change the people's approaches, values, and beliefs and also encourages them to family planning and birth-control. Majority of the respondents believed that there are strong links between women's education and their employment and income.

Majority believed that jobs for women are important because a job makes women financially independent and helps the family economy. And they believed both man and woman should participate in earning money.

Amongst the respondents, some of the women believed that there are disadvantages of women's employment because when they are working outside, they will not have enough time to look after children because they are busy and tired. Also they haven't enough time for their husbands.

Among the respondents more than half stated teaching is a good occupation, because teacher has good and superior position among the people. Also, there is more free time and more holidays as compared to other jobs. So they have more time to be at home and perform their duty fowards their families. And some of the women were interested in other occupations, such as: banking, being a physician or government officer because of financial support, good income and social status.

In this study, respondents stated that sometimes they suffer disadvantages in the offices because of their gender. They added that they could hardly agree with women being in senior positions or boss. Besides; they imagine women are unable to do great work. This shows evidence of traditional male thinking about the workplace and the role of women in it, in contrast to the more modern idea.

Recently, Iran has witnessed a more modern phenomenon

in the household: the two-income family. That means that both husband and wife are earning salary. There are certainly both advantages and disadvantages in this mode. Although the family mentioned has certain advantages, such as the blending of roles, it faces pressures arising from the traditional division of labour between men and women in the family structure along with the new responsibilities of those members. This problem needs to be managed properly or it may have negative impact on both social unity and the function of the family, as well as on the mental health and social lives of the members.

The researcher noted that, in this study that the majority responded that they spend their salary by contributing to family income for everyday life. Whereas the slender minority responded that they use their salaries to provide personal benefits, such as personal needs or giving to their own parents.

In the present study, to establish a balance between house and office, the respondents have regular time tables to work at home and office. Sometimes their husbands or parents help them to take care of children and home duty or they have servants at home.

They stated their work could help the family income and it improves family economic situation. Therefore they can provide more facilities for family growth and progress.

In addition, financial independence makes them powerful and influential, and they can share their income in family welfare. Whereas the economic situation is important for family, women employment has positive role in family stability.

This research shows women's employment as influence to the family power structure. Education increases direct and indirect costs and economic benefits. Women's social status would lead to major changes in socio-economical variables in the country. Almost all the respondents state that job is important because it makes 'family stability' and helps 'family economy'.

Majority of the respondents believe that financial independence has a great impact. Because of financial independence, women can participate in family decision making; even sometimes they are more powerful than their husbands, and their income helps the family welfare and women feel calm. Owing to the present economic situation in Iranian society with the high cost of living, it is difficult for men to provide the family with all necessities.

Additionally, the power structure of patriarchy within families, women's greater awareness, their social participation, employment and education, will transform their status in the family and society.

Almost all women belonging to different occupations such as: business persons, clerks, teachers, physicians, engineers, lawyers, university teachers, government officers, university students, were satisfied with their job and were totally happy and pleased.

According to Myron Weiner (1971), women's advancement in society pivots on their participation in politics. Women must voice their needs and opinions in order to receive the needed changes in society and in their lives. But simultaneously, these changes are essential for women to gain access to socio-political power and influence.

Moreover, the researcher found out women had political participation such as: canvassing, agitations, political meeting, and hunger strikes; also, majority of women had participated in voting regularly.

Furthermore, respondents believe that education, political experience, crime-free record, party manifesto, cast/religion are important criteria's in electing a candidate in political activities.

In addition, the study shows that most of the women, living in the research location, had participated in provincial activities such as public utility, social security, social election, provincial and urban and rural election, economic activities, social activities, religious socialization, political involvement, ethnic or provincial ceremonies, and so on.

Majority of the respondents predict lots of changes in both quality and quantity of politics if women participated in politics such as: decline of corruption, increase of people's belief in politics, reduction of political criminalization, and decrease in men's traditional authority towards women and their increased participation will provide greater self-confidence in women, as a result women's problems will be settled.

Majority of the women under study believed that some factors characterize traditional women, such as: good mother, good wife, family supporter. The characteristics of modern women not only are good mother, good wife, and family supporter, which are characteristics of traditional women; but there are also additional characteristics such as: education, vote depended, outdoor worker, independent women which depicts modern women. The virtue and wearing *hejab* are characteristics of religious women. The characteristics of a religious woman encompass the features of both modern and traditional women. We can see that all of women's characteristics are important in the community.

Religion is defined as a system of symbols designed to produce powerful and longlasting moods and motivation in men, which is rooted in facts and viewed as realistic. Geertz (1975) defined it as a cultural universal around which all other institutions are integrated. It is an aspect of culture which serves humanity; but, whenever a society is dissatisfied with that religion, the members tend to change their religion (conversion). This happens when the old religion cannot adapt to suit the needs of the people. One such religion is Islam, an Arabic word referring to both peace and submission.

Since the majority of the population in Iran are Muslim and nearly half of the population are women, women's religious activities are more important. Most of the women living in Tonekabon city, had participated in both public and private religious ceremonies. Public religious ceremonies include those programs which are performed in streets, mosques, and other public places. Private religious ceremonies include those programs that are performed at home or some private places where men are not allowed to enter. Of course elder women are more active in religious programs.

All respondents believe in God, resurrection, soul, hell, heaven, and ghost. And a God influences the individual's social and private life and it leads to the acceptance of religious beliefs and is followed by the improvement in moral and religious values.

The present study shows that most of the respondents pray to God by "Namaz". And "Namaz" is the name for the compulsory prayers which are performed five times a day, and it is a direct link between the worshipper and the God with no earthly intermediaries. A prayer takes a few minutes to be performed.

Prayer, obligatory and spontaneous, is an enormous spiritual treasure to be valued. It encourages peace, purity and tranquillity and instils companionship with God.

In this study, respondents believed in Norooz (New Year) ceremony that is very important, because that is an old custom. And Norooz is a symbol of ancient Persia and brings hope, friendship, peace, tranquillity, success and prosperity to the world especially in Persia. The first day of spring is the beginning of Norooz. Before spring, Iranian people prepare themselves for Norooz by cleaning their homes. Most of the wedding parties in Iran are held during the Norooz holiday which is two weeks.

A vital function of a religious ceremony is to explain the meaning and aspects of a physical and social environment which may not be fully understood via normal thoughts and experiences.

This research shows that women believed in pilgrim's

ceremony, because they are Muslim and they follow all Islamic ceremonies. In such ceremonies, pilgrims go to religious places in cities of Iran such as Mashhad and Ghom to pray. Some people believe that if they visit pilgrimage places and ask God to cure some diseases, their prayer will be fulfilled; in other words, God will answer their prayers. In addition to this there are two important cities such as Mecca and Medina in Saudi Arabia. Every year lots of pilgrims go there to perform the religious ceremony.

K. N. Dash (2004) defined marriage as a social institution. By means of this institution, men and women can satisfy their biological needs in an acceptable manner. It is universal because it fulfils both: one vital social function and reproduction while regulating the sexual relationship. In the modern world, no society exists in which marriage in any form is absent.

In the present study, most of the respondents under study believed that women's marriage is important, because a woman can have married life and she can be a good mother and a good wife; furthermore, marriage is important according to Islam for life cycle to continue. Marriage and family are complementary concepts. Marriage is an institution and family is the association that embodies the institution. Marriage has existed in every form of society from time immemorial. Based on Iranian scriptures, marriage system in Iran was well established in Zoroastrian Period. From ancient times, marriage is considered as a ritual and sacramental union.

In this study, majority of respondents believed in marriage 'Khastegari' that is wooing custom. According to them, that is important custom because wooing is a traditional custom. Through this 'wooing custom' two members of the family will become more familiar with each other and it is the way to fasten the family friendship.

Also about the "Namzadi", that is engagement custom, respondents said this is important because it is a kind of marriage celebration and makes pleasure and memorable time for both couples and families. The "engagement custom" is held after the "wooing custom" in which the groom's family gives gifts like a ring, clothes and cookies or sweets to the bride. In "engagement custom" the close relatives of both sides of the two families are invited.

The respondents feel that Aghd, marriage contract custom, is also important, because it is an official contract between man and woman as a couple and, according to Islam, marriage contract should be written officially. Also, they believed that marriage contract develops and increases stability of common life.

Majority believed that Mahrieh, marriage payments custom, is important because "Mahrieh" "payment" is a gift from the groom for the bride and it is given in the form of money or gold coins. The amount of this money is a source of financial security for married women in case of divorce or widowhood.

Most of the respondents believed on the Sheer Bahaa, bride price, custom. They said that it is important because it is custom of agreement upon money or gift given to the bride's family. "Bride price" is a gift to the bride's mother for having nursed her. Now part of the marriage portion settled upon the wife is paid beforehand in cash.

The women, under study, attached great importance to education and income and have shown a strong, positive, attitude towards education and income. They consider education and income as a key to change and one of the important forces in building their status.

In the present study we can conclude that there is a change in the lifestyle of leisure time activities, socio-economic life, educational life, political life of the women in Tonekabon city. In addition to this there is also change in the attitude toward vital characteristics of women. But there is no change in the attitude toward the religion and religious activities, some traditional ceremonies, religious ceremonies, traditional customs and believes in marriage ceremony. Therefore we can say that there is a change in the lifestyle as long as material culture is concerned but there is not much change in the lifestyle of non-material culture of women in Tonekabon city.

# References

## Books (English)

Anderson, Nels. 1961. Man's *Work and Leisure.* London: Routledge.

Beattie, J. 1964. *Other Culture: Aims, Methods and Achievements in Social Anthropology*. New York: The Free Press of Glencoe.

Bourdieu, Pierre. 1984. *Distinction; A Social Critique of the Judgement of Taste*. Trans. by Richard Nice. London: Routledge and Kegan Paul Ltd.

__________. 1990. *In Other Words: Essays Towards a Reflexive Sociology*. Trans. by Matthew Adamson, Cambridge: Polity Press.

er, Marilynn B. and Hewstone, Miles. 2004. *Self and Social Identity*. ılden, MA: Blackwell Publishing.

ıghtbill, Charles Kestner. 1960. *The Challenge of Leisure*. Englewood Cliffs, NJ: Prentice- Hall.

Brothers, Jain. 1984. *Social Profile of Working Women*. Delhi: Varshney Printing Press.

Carlson, Reynold E. 1972. *Recreation in American Life*. Belmont, Calif.: Wadsworth Publishing Company.

Carroll, Theodora Foster. 1983. *Women, Religion, and Development in the Third World*. New York: Praeger Publishers.

Chaney, D. 1996. *Lifestyle*. London: Routledge.

Charbonneau, Johanne and Gauthier, Madeleine. Fall 2001. "Introduction Culture and Lifestyle." Quebec: University Press of Quebec, Vol. 24, issue 2, p. 349-617.

Crawford, Mary and Unger, Rhoda. 2000. *Women and Gender*. New York: McGraw-Hill Company.

Dahl G. J. 1972. *Time, Work and Leisure*. New York: Christian Century Foundation.

Dash, K. N. 2004. *Invitation to Social and Cultural Anthropology*. Delhi: Nice Printing Press.

Desai, Vandana and Potter, Robert B.eds. 2002. *The Companion to Development Studies*. London and New York: Oxford University Press.

Devis, Kinsley, 1950. *Human Society*. New York: Macmillan.

Dumazedier, J. and Ripert, A. 1967. *Toward a Society of Leisure*. London: Collier-Macmillan.

Epstein, S. 1973. *The Self-concept Revisited, or a Theory of Theory*. American Psychologist, Vol. 28. pp. 404-16.

Evelyn Ashton-Jones Gary A. Olson, Merry G. Perry. 2000. *The Gender Reader*. Boston: Allyn and Bacon

Fairchild, H.P., 1944. ed., *Philosophical Library*, New York: McGraw- Hill.

Gardner, Katy and Lewis, David. 1996. *Anthropology, Development and the Post-modern Challenge*. London: Pluto Press.

Geertz, 1975. *Anthropological Study of Religion*. In "International Encyclopaedia of the Social Sciences". David, L. Sellis (ed), New York: Macmillan company and the free press Vol-13-14.

Ghurge G. S. 1963. *Anthropo-Sociological Papers*. Bombay: Bhatkal.

Giddens, Anthony. 1990. *The Consequences of Modernity*. Stanford, California: Stanford University Press.

Giddens, Anthony. 1994. *Sociology*, Cambridge: Polity Press.

Gilbert, Allon and Gugler, Josef 1981 *Cities, Poverty and Development*. ELBS

Gist, NP. and Fava, SF. 1964. *Urban Society*. New York: Crowell.

Gupta, Amit Kumar. 1986. *Women and Society the Developmental Perspective*. New Delhi: Mayapuri.

Harrison, David. 1988. *The Sociology of Modernization and Development*. London: Unwin Hyman Ltd.

Havighurst, R. J. 1957. *The Leisure Activities of the Middle Aged. American Journal of Sociology*.

Hoebel E. A. 1958. *Anthropology, The Study of Man*. New York: McGraw Hill.

Jena, Sanjay Ketan. 1993. *Working Women and Modernization*. New Delhi: Ashish Publishing House.

Jha, Kali Nath. 1985. *Women toward Modernization*. New Delhi: Nand Kishore Singh.

Kaplan, M. 1960. *Leisure in America*. New York: Wiley.

Korzenny, Felipe. 1992. ed. *Mass Media Effects Across Cultures*. London: Sage Publications.

Kurane, Anjali. 1991. *Ethnic Identity and Social Mobility*. New Delhi: Rawat Publications.

____________. 2002. *Socio-Cultural Changes Among The 'Mahadeo-Kolis' In Maharashtra,* The Oriental Anthropologist 2 (1).

Larrabee Eric, Meyersohn Rolf. 1958. (eds.), *Mass Leisure.* Glencoe, Illinois: Free Press.

Lerner, D. 1966. *The Passing of Traditional Society: Modernising the Middle East.* New York: The Free Press of Gllencoe.

Mahajan, V. S. 1989. *Women's Contribution to India's Economic and Social Development.* New Delhi: Deep and Deep Publications.

Mann, Peter H. 1965. An Approach to Urban Sociology. London: EC. 4.

McCormack, Thelma, 1971. "Politics and Leisure". Articles in the *International Journal of Comparative Sociology,* September, pp. 169-81.

Meyersohn R. 1972. ed. *The Human Meaning of Social Chane.* New York: Russell Sage Foundation.

Miller and Robinson. 1963. *The Leisure Age: Its Challenge to Recreation.*

*Miller, Elmer S. and Weitz, Charles A. 1979.* Introduction to Anthropology. *Englewood Cliffs, N.J.: Prentice-Hall.*

Modi, Ishwar. 1985. *Leisure Mass Media and Social Structure.* Jaipur: Rewat Publications.

Moor, H. 1989. *Feminism and Anthropology.* Minneapolis: University of Minnesota Press.

Mpmsen, Janet Henshall. 1996. *Women and Development in the Third World.* London: Routledge.

Nadel, S. F. 1953. *Anthropology and Modlife.* Canberra: Australian National University Press.

Ogburn, W. F. 1966. *Social Change.* New York: Dell.

Parker, Stanley. 1976. *The Sociology of Leisure.* London: George Allen and Unwin Ltd.

Panda, N. K. 2006. *Policies Programmes and Strategies for Tribal Development.* Delhi: Kalpaz Publication.

Pelto, P.J. 1972. "Research Strategies in the Study of Complex Societies." In Weaver, T, and White, D. (ed.). *The Anthropology of Urban Environment.* SAA Monograph, Washington: Society for Applied Anthropology.

Piddington, R. 1956. *An Introduction to Social Anthropology.* Edinburgh: Oliver and Boyd.

Reissman, Leonard. 1954. Class, Leisure, and Social Participation. *American Sociological Review.* Vol. 19. (Fall 1954)

Rojek, C. 2000. *Leisure and Culture.* Basingstoke, Hants.: Macmillan.

Rojek, C. 1985. *Capitalism and Leisure Theory*. London: Tavvistock.

Sanjay, Ketan Jena. 1993. *Working Women and Modernization*. New Delhi: Ashish Publication House.

Sharabi, H. 1988. Neopatriarchy, A Theory of Distorted Change in Arab Society. New York: Oxford University Press.

Skevington, Suzanne and Baker, Deborah. 1989. *The Social Identity of Women*. London: Sage Publication.

Smelser, N. J. 1967. ed. *Sociology.* New York: Wiley.

Sunder, D. Raj. 2006. *Group Dynamics and Women.* In the "Empowering Rule India" R. Ravi, P. Siva, D. Sunder Raj. New Delhi.

Talwar, Usha. 1984. *Social Profile of Working Women*. Jodhpur: Jain Brothers.

Touraine, A. 1974. *The Post-Industrial*. London: Wildwood House.

Tylor, E. B. 1999. Dictionary *of Anthropology.* Delhi: Jawaharlal Nagar.

Unger, R. K. 1978. The Politis of Gender: A review of relevant literature. In J. Sherman and F. Denmark (eds), *Psychology of Women: Future Directions of Research.*

Veal, A. J. 1987. The Leisure Forecasting Tradition. In *Leisure and the Future*. London: Allen and Unwin.

Vivelo, F. R. 1978. *Cultural Anthropology: A Basic Introduction*. New York: University Press of America.

Wallance, Anthony F. C. 1966. *Religion: An Anthropological View.* New York: Random House.

Woods, Tim. 2000. *Theorizing Modernity*. London: Oxford University Press.

Webster, Noah. 1963. *Webster's Dictionary*. New York: The World Publishing Company.

Weeks, Jeffry and Holland, Janet. 1996. *Sexual Cultures Communities, Values and Intimacy*. British Sociological Association.

Weiner, Myron. 1971. *Political Participant: Crisis and Sequence in Political Development*. Princeton: Princeton University Press.

Yoder, Janice D. 1999. *Women and Gender*. Prentice- Hall, Inc.

Zaltman Gerald and Duncan Robert. 1977. *Strategies for Planned Change.* New York: A Willey-Interscience Publication.

## Books (Persian)

Azadarmaki,Taghi and Ghyasvand Ahmad. 2003. *Sociology of Culture Changes in Iran*. Tehran: AN Publications.

Fakouhi, Nasser. 2003. *Urban Anthropology*. Tehran: Ney Publication.

Giddens, Anthony. 1990. *Sociology*. Trans. by Manocher Mohseni, Tehran: Mehr Publication.

Kazemi, Ali Asghar. 1997. *Crisis in Modern Society*. Tehran: The Centre of Islamic Culture Publication.

Mohseni, Manocher. 1995. *Sociology Introduction*. Tehran: Davaran Publication.

Roshe, G. 1969. *Social Change*. Trans. by Mansor Vosoghye, Tehran: Ney Publication.

**Journals (Persian)**

Amini, Alireza. Spring 2004. "Gender Approach to Imbalances in the Labour Market". *Pazhuhish-i Zanan*, Vol. 2, No.1, p.133.

Azad Armaki, Taghi and Chavoshian Hassan. Winter 2003. "The Human Body as a Medium of Identity." *Iranian Journal of Sociology*, Vol.1, No. 4, p. 57.

Elmi, Zahra. Summer 2004. "Macro-Economic Policies and the Labour Market for Women in Iran." *Pazhuhish-i Zanan*, Vol. 2, No.2, p.17.

Enayat, Halima and Movahed Majid. Summer 2004. "Women and Structural Transformations in Family in the Era of Globalization." *Pazhuhish-i Zanan*, Vol. 2, No. 2, p. 153.

Fakouhi, Nasser and Mirdamadi, Mehrdad. Fall and Winter 2003. "Cyberspace as Urban Space in Tehran." *Iranian Journal of Anthropology*, Vol.1, No. 2, p. 89.

Fakouhi, Nasser and Ansari, Fereshteh. Fall and Winter 2002. "Leisure Time and Cultural Personality Formation in Two Girls' High School in the City of Tehran'. *Iranian Journal of Anthropology*, Vol. 1, No. 4, p. 61.

Fakouhi Nasser, Parsapajouh, Sepideh. Spring and Summer 2002. "Formation of Cultural Identity among Teenage Girls of Islamabad, Karaj." *Iranian Journal of Anthropology*, Vol.1, No.1, p.123.

Mirzaie Hossein, Spring 2004. "Factors Impacting Iranian Women's Economic Participation." Pazhuhish-i Zanan, Vol. 2, No.1, p.113.

Mirzadeh, H. 2003. "Factors in the Women's Engagement in Economical Activities in Iran." *Pazhuhish-I Zanan*, Vol. 2, No.1.

Neekpay, Amir. 2000. "A Reviewing of Certain Religious Changes in Contemporary Iran." *Journal of the Iranian Sociological Association*; Especial Issue of the Social Problem in Iran. No.3.

Sadeghi, Masoud and Emadzadeh, Mostafa. Spring 2004. *"An Analysis of Economic Factors Affecting Women's Employment in Iran."* Vol. 2, No. 1, p.5.

Safi, M. and M. Emadzadeh. 2003. "The Impact of Economical Factors on Women Employment in Iran." *Pazhuhish-i Zanan*, Vol. 2. No.1.

Saroukhani, Bagher and Rafatjah, Maryam. Spring 2004. "Sociological Factors Related to the Re-definition of Women's Social Identity." Tehran: *Pazhuhish-i Zanan*, Vol. 2, No, 1, p. 71.

Shaditalab, Jaleh. June 2004. "Rural Women's Bank of Hesarbone: The Outcome of a Participatory Approach." *Women's Research: Journal of the Centre for Women's Studies*, Vol.1, No.1, p. 57.

Shirodi, Morteza. Summer 2005. *"Social-political Role of Women in Contemporary Iran."* Vol. 3, No.2, p. 75.

**Thesis (Persian)**

Abedinizadeh, Narges. 1993. "How Higher School Girls in 17th area of Tehran Spend Their Leisure Time." M. A. Thesis. Tehran: University of Tehran, Department of Anthropology.

Behzadian, Nejad Nasiba. 2004. 'Beauty and Culture.' Ph.D. Thesis. Tehran: University of Tehran, Department of Sociology.

Elyasi, Mahzad. 2004. "Girls Cultural Anthropology Survey." M.A. Thesis. Tehran: University of Tehran, Department of Anthropology.

Mahdizade, Sharare. 2001. "T.V. and Innovation". Ph.D. Thesis. Tehran: University of Tehran, Department of Sociology.

Sasgarnejad, Parvin. 2002. "Investigates on University Professor and Traditional Businessmen." Ph.D. Thesis. Tehran: University of Tehran, Department of Sociology.

Sharbatian, Mohammad Hassan. 2000. "A Comparative Study of the Life Style of the Students of Art, Boys of 18 to 25 years old in Cultural Centre of Bahman and Amir Kabir." M. A. Thesis. Tehran: University of Tehran, Department of Anthropology.

Zalnejad, Farzane. 1991. "How 11th Standard School Girls in 17th and third area of Tehran Spend their leisure time." M.A. Thesis. Tehran: University of Tehran, Department of Sociology.

## Online Sources

Anthony. Veal (2001), <www.puq.uquebec.ca>

Alvin Toffler. < http://en.wikipedia.org/wiki/Leisure_time>

# Index